"My childhood was not all suffering. It was not all slum. I was always *well* dressed, *well* fed, *well* schooled, and brought up to be a nice lower-middle-class English boy. And that's what made the Beatles different, the fact that George, Paul, and John were *grammar* school boys."

"Strawberry Fields is a Salvation Army home that was near the house I lived in with my Auntie in the suburbs. Apparently, it used to be a farm that made strawberries or whatever. But I just took the name as an image—Strawberry Fields forever."

"Mahatma Gandhi and Martin Luther King are great examples of fantastic nonviolents who died violently. I can never work that out. We're pacifists, but I'm not sure what it means when you're such a pacifist that you get shot. I can never understand *that*."

"I can't walk away from the Beatles. That's one possession that's still tagging along, right? If I walk away from what I am, whether it's two houses or four hundred houses, I'm not gonna escape it."

"I'm not running for office. I'm not gonna curtail everything I say to fit some image of myself or to fit some fantasy of somebody else's image of me. If you can't stand the heat, get out of the pissoir!"

THE **PLAYBOY** INTERVIEWS WITH

JOHN LENNON & YOKO ONO

CONDUCTED BY DAVID SHEFF
EDITED BY G. BARRY GOLSON

BERKLEY BOOKS, NEW YORK

This Berkley book contains the complete
text of the original hardcover edition.
It has been completely reset in a typeface
designed for easy reading, and was printed
from new film.

THE PLAYBOY INTERVIEWS WITH
JOHN LENNON AND YOKO ONO

A Berkley Book / published by arrangement with
the author

PRINTING HISTORY
Playboy Press edition / August 1981
Berkley edition / December 1982

ISBN: 0-425-05989-8

Foreword

"This will be the reference book," John Lennon said wryly to the reporter and the magazine editor near the end of twenty hours of conversations taped during three weeks in September 1980. He was speaking figuratively, of course, because the tapes were intended as background for the interview that would appear in PLAYBOY in December. It was already apparent that there was far more material than even the lengthy Playboy Interview could accommodate (it eventually ran at 20,000 words), but Lennon seemed eager to continue talking. And when it was proposed to him that he go over his entire musical output, song by song, as a way to spur his memories, he agreed enthusiastically. "We'll do the whole damn thing," he said. "You can do it from the womb to the grave. *Boom!*"

Later that September afternoon, the editor remarked, "You'll only have to do this once in your life, John." Lennon looked up tiredly and said, "Yeah, in my life."

With hindsight, anyone can read portents and meanings into what Lennon said that day—or on other days, for that matter, since Lennon talked often about life and death. But what seemed undeniable to us even then was that these interview sessions were something special to him. It was the first time in five years that he and his wife, Yoko Ono, had spoken with the outside world, and he had stored up a lot of things to say. He was giving a few other, shorter interviews to promote their new record album. But the PLAYBOY sessions, for whatever reasons, were evidently the means he had chosen to sum it *all* up—the Beatles, his former partners, his own childhood, the seeds of rebellion and artistry, the creation of the music itself, the relationship with Yoko, and much he'd come to learn about politics and sexual roles and creativity and passion . . . and why men of peace are inevitably killed.

The magazine interview had been on the newsstands only a few days when the murder occurred in the archway of the Dakota in New York City on December 8. In the worldwide outpouring of grief, the interview was one vehicle by which people could share something of the man—his music, of course, being the main source.

But within a few days, the magazine became impossible to find on the nation's newsstands, and mail poured into the magazine's offices requesting copies that were no longer available. Because the magazine represented at least a name and an address for people reacting to the tragedy, hundreds of readers wrote that they had actually been reading the interview that evening as they heard the news about Lennon, and they had to have someone, or something, to whom they could pour out their emotions. Even a short follow-up article on Lennon's music, already in the works but published several months later, was not enough to satisfy those who wanted to know more about the man who had changed a generation.

For David Sheff, Lennon's interviewer, and for me, as the editor involved, there was another frustration. Because of the space problems inherent in any magazine, we had left so much out that Lennon had said—so many memories and ideas and funny, off-the-cuff remarks from someone who would never be heard from again. (At the beginning of one session, Lennon greeted Sheff at the door of his apartment singing, to the tune of "Eleanor Rigby," "Here's David Sheff, come to ask questions with answers that no one will hear." A joke, of course, but one we remembered later.) And amid the spate of books about Lennon in the months after his death, it didn't seem appropriate to simply dole out other parts of the conversations in bits and pieces.

Thus, the decision to publish this book. Not merely to reprint the original edited interview and the article summarizing his musical output, but *all* of it—or at least as much of the conversations as seemed to have enduring value. We have returned to the original tapes and descriptive notes and attempted to reconstruct our conversations with John and Yoko. There has been editing for clarity and brevity, of course—the actual transcripts would take up several volumes—but two-thirds of the material in this book has never been published before.

To Sheff, and other people in their twenties, Lennon represented a symbol beyond music or pop mythology. When, during a casual conversation in the summer of 1980, I gave him the assignment to track down the elusive Lennons Sheff's excitement went beyond the bounds of the normal magazine project. For the members of his generation, Lennon has been the artist who had refused to give up, whose music and lyrics and life cut through the complacency of the post-Sixties torpor. It was to him, and others like him, that Lennon had seemed to address the words in "Strawberry Fields Forever": "Living *is* easy with eyes closed, misunderstanding all you see. . . ."

To me, and to those of us in our thirties and early forties, he was family. He was the brilliant brother who did it all—created great music, achieved unparalleled success and fame, played along the cliff edges of drugs and sex and self-destruction—then talked with compulsive honesty about it, sometimes foolishly, often painfully, but always returning home to share what he'd learned.

So it seemed to us that Lennon had given us a legacy that should be repaid. We were, quite by chance, the recipients of what people close to Lennon would later call his "final testament." *Los Angeles Times* arts editor Charles Champlin wrote of the published magazine interview, "David Sheff's sympathetic questions evoked so much of the Beatle past and of Lennon's intellectual past and present and future plans that the interview would hardly have been less engrossing and important even if it were not illuminated by tragedy.'' Perhaps, but the tragedy illuminated for us the fact that we would not see Lennon's like again, and that the complete conversations deserved to be shared and preserved. A previous interview with Lennon, published in *Rolling Stone* in 1971, gave the public an insight into Lennon at his most anguished. This interview, with Lennon in a reflective and happy period in his life, should round out the portrait fully.

Jay Cocks, writing the cover story for *Time* magazine that week in December, referred to the PLAYBOY interview as ''lively proof that some of the best Lennon/Ono art was their life,'' and concluded his piece movingly: ''Lennon could have gone the way of Elvis Presley, could have destroyed himself. But he did something harder. He lived. And, for all the fame and finance, that seemed to be what he took the most pride in. . . . That was the victory Mark Chapman took from John Lennon, who had an abundance of what everybody wants and wanted only what so many others have, and take for granted. A home and family. Some still center of love. A life. One minute more.''

This book, we hope, is a few minutes more.

G. BARRY GOLSON
Executive Editor
PLAYBOY
New York, 1981

Introduction

When I was asked in the early summer of 1980 to find out whether John Lennon and Yoko Ono would sit for a Playboy Interview, I took it as a challenge without realizing the door I was opening.

I began placing calls to friends who might know something. I arranged to see people known to have hung out with the Lennons—musical figures like Harry Nilsson, and Phil Spector and Nicky Hopkins, anyone who might lead me to the reclusive couple. Jakob Magnussen, an extraordinary jazz musician I had once written about, called to tell me the surprising and still-secret news: John was contacting musicians—Earl Slick, Hugh McCracken, Andy Newmark, and others—and had hired a producer, Jack Douglas, to record an album.

The odyssey began. I left countless messages for Douglas to call. When he finally did, I was out. In the meantime, I got the phone number of a publicist reportedly working with Yoko Ono. He was the one who released a news item about Yoko's quarter-of-a-million-dollar cow sale. Another phone number led me to the Lennons' accountant, a gentle man who seemed to want me to at least have a chance to get to his bosses. He promised that a letter from me would get Yoko's personal attention, and I carefully composed a telegram. I continued to pursue other contacts: the other musicians, Douglas, all kinds of strange leads. I went to New York and met with anyone who even hinted he could possibly help. I met three or four people who each claimed to be the sole door to the Lennons. Back in California, I was told that the Boston publicist had called. Yoko received my telegram. A meeting was set. I was to see Yoko at the Dakota.

One of Yoko's assistants called to ask for the time and place of my birth. The interview apparently depended on Yoko's interpretation of my horoscope, just as many of the Lennons' business decisions are reportedly guided by the stars. I could imagine explaining to my PLAYBOY editor, Barry Golson, "Sorry, but my moon is in Scorpio—the interview's off." It was clearly out of my hands. I supplied the information: December 23, 3:00 P.M., Boston.

I wasn't sure what to expect as I entered the Dakota, past the ominous gates and numerous security checkpoints, on September 8. In the outer office, I met two of the voices that had become familiar on the telephone: Richard DePalma, the accountant; and Fred Seaman, a friend and assistant to John and Yoko. They were consistently gracious and helpful. One asked me to remove my shoes before entering Yoko's private office.

Yoko was on the telephone when I entered, but she nodded and signaled for me to sit down on the couch near her. I sat straight, sizing her up. She seemed, as I anticipated, severe.

We chatted—New York, the weather, the plane flight. She darted to the next topic. Besides my astrological sign, she had read my numbers. Based on them both, she concluded, "This is a very important time for you. This interview will mean more than you can comprehend now." Did that mean we were on? Never a straight answer. She was testing me. I answered questions about my conception of the interview, some of my own preconceptions I hoped to clear up. She was not impressed with the importance I obviously gave the interview; that was taken for granted. I suggested she examine previous Playboy Interviews and promised to drop samples off. She told me to call her the next morning.

That afternoon I dropped off copies of past interviews with Jimmy Carter, Martin Luther King, Bob Dylan, Albert Schweitzer, and others. The heavy artillery. The next morning I called the Dakota and asked for Yoko. "Why don't you meet me here at noon?" she asked.

At the Dakota, there was a message for me to meet Yoko at a nearby coffeehouse. Soon I found myself sitting across a couple of cups of cappuccino from John Lennon. John was apparently just up, bleary-eyed and unshaven, sipping coffee while waiting for Yoko, who was busy on the telephone. "It's too early for any of this," he said smiling. "I don't know how she does it."

After small talk and coffee, Yoko directed us to the limousine. We began to get acquainted in the car as it headed through the west side of town, squeezing down crowded streets. John, balanced on the jump seat at Yoko's feet, which were resting on his lap, explained what the day was to hold. The final song on the album was to be Yoko's "Hard Times Are Over (for a While)." A gospel background was to be recorded.

Yoko, vaguely reading the *New York Times* through her ever-present dark sunglasses, glanced up at John, whose head was perched up against the car's window. John's army-green jacket was unbuttoned, its collar turned up around his neck. Underneath was a plain white T-shirt. He held on to the armrest and the driver's seat in front of him for balance. Yoko, whose jet-black hair, tied tightly back, blended with her black leather jacket, folded the *Times* up and stowed it on the seat next to her. John's thoughts were apparently on the pending interviews, for his next words were directed to me. "I'm looking forward to this," he said. "It's been a long time since we've done this kind of thing." He spoke excitedly. "First thing, you've got to hear the music. Wait till you hear the music! We'll play the tape for you later."

When we arrived at the studio—an old warehouse chosen for the day's session primarily because of its cavernous space—the crew, including producer Jack Douglas, engineer Lee DeCarlo, and a handful of assistants, were already in the control room. John quickly greeted the group, and in the same breath introduced me around the room. Douglas smiled when he recognized my name, and winked. "Congratulations," he said with the implied but unstated addendum: "I never expected to meet you, but welcome."

Douglas took what turned out to be his customary seat in front of the control board flanked by three chairs, two on one side waiting for John and Yoko, and one on his other side for DeCarlo. Seated in that same configuration at this studio or the regular one, the Hit Factory, the four looked like engineers at some hip NASA, preparing for a rocket launch.

Yoko told me to make myself comfortable and had one of her assistants, a Japanese boy named Toshi Hamaya, get her and John cups of English breakfast tea with milk, and coffee for me.

On the other side of the glass partition, the Benny Cummings Singers and the Kings Temple Choir were warming up with the project's arranger, Tony Davilio. After Tony played the chorus to "Hard Times Are Over" on the piano, Cummings expertly broke his group up into vocal sections, which were soon harmonizing the choral, churchlike "hmmmms" and "ooohhhs" that would fill in Yoko's song. On the first run-through with the taped version of the song playing as the lead track, John looked up quite pleased with the strange mixture of soulful black choir wailing over Yoko's eccentric, high-pitched vocals with their Oriental accent. Lennon said, "Here must be the world's first Japanese gospel song."

Douglas and the others rewound tape, switched switches, and turned nobs, and John turned to the control room's mike and switched it on so the choir, behind the glass, could hear him. He spoke in the unmistakable Lennon voice, welcoming the group and thanking them for coming. We lip-read thank-yous through the glass. Jack and John nodded to each other to signal their readiness and John laughed into the mike: "Well, let's make some music."

Over the control room's monitors, switched on so the choir could be heard, came a roar of "Thank you, thank you Jesus" and "Amen, amen, amen." When John realized that the group was beautifully and spontaneously praying, he whispered to DeCarlo, "Get that on two-track, quick!" The prayer was recorded. It is the opening of "Hard Times Are Over (for a While)."

John listened to the first run-throughs intently while he sipped the second cup of tea Toshi gracefully served. Whether it was a minutely out-of-tune tenor or an unnoticeable (to me) pause between two of the song's bars, John calmly and consistently broke into the recording session to ask for another try. "Clearer enunciation of the final 'over,' " he would call out. "Try not dropping the second syllable. Try 'o—ver' sustained, rather than 'o—ver' descending," he said, singing both versions himself. At times he would seem to lose himself in the music, but he never missed even the smallest detail. As the music boomed over the monitor speakers, John swayed with Yoko's taped voice, silently mouthing the lyrics as they played. Then he glanced in my direction to catch me watching him. He winked and asked, "Well, what do you think?"

When the passionate chorus completely surrounded Yoko's reedy, piccololike singing, it sounded more like a prayer than a pop song. John asked for the result to be played back for everyone to hear. It was, and it all sounded marvelous. The song had become full and whole, as Yoko had conceived it. John looked at her and found her eyes filled with tears. He leaned his chair back on its swivel so he could reach over her shoulder. "Pretty nice, mother," he said. Yoko nodded, wiping free-flowing tears with her sleeve.

Hours later, when the track was down and John and Yoko had recorded the chorus chanting, as per her instructions, the four words "ONE WORLD, ONE PEOPLE," over and over again as a possible ending to the album, Cummings asked if his group might thank the Lennons with a song. Afterwards, John expressed his own appreciation to the group and personally made sure an assistant had the correct spelling of its name for album credits. He accepted kisses and handshakes as the entourage left the studio. Of course there was the requisite question. One of the singers asked, "How's Paul?" John amiably laughed, "Paul who?"

The air in the limo was fresh and lively. "It's working nicely, dear, isn't it?" John asked, happy and inspired. "What a gift we were given! Well, next stop, sir, the Hit Factory."

A plate full of specially prepared sushi and sashimi, teriyaki chicken and vegetables waited on the fifth floor of the West Side recording studio, a much more modern enterprise where the secure top floor is reserved for special projects. A big black man stood guard over the floor.

While John and the others munched a few pieces of fish and talked about the morning's session, Yoko opened her briefcase and carefully withdrew loose-leaf pages with scribbled words on them—the tentative lyrics to the songs that would become *Double Fantasy*. She told me I should read them later. "Now," she said, "I'll show you around."

Yoko guided me to a lounge stocked with teas and coffees and Hershey bars, and then to the control room itself. There was a couch in front of the control panel where I could rest as they worked. A chair had been placed behind their own so I could view all the goings-on. In addition to the lounge, there was a special room— Yoko's room—which was quiet, carpeted, and was decorated with Japanese prints, exotic fresh flowers—orchids and single fantasy freesias (double fantasies were impossible to get that time of year)—and a luxurious couch. She explained that I could get away from the noise there, that she and John used the room to get away and rest during the sessions.

We returned to the main studio, where John and the others were busy working on the day's tape. I watched for several hours before Yoko suggested we leave. In the car, John asked if I was ready to begin the interview back at the apartment. ''We'll go until you get—until we *all* get satisfied,'' he said.

DAVID SHEFF

PART ONE

1

At the Dakota, the elderly guard, more a fixture than a comfort in front of the gray, ghostly apartment house, opened the car doors for us. John greeted the man by name and hastily but gently smiled for some snapshots posed with a fan who had been waiting up late just on the off chance of meeting him. After two quick flashes of the bulbs, John blindly headed for the entryway. Blinking to regain his eyesight, he stopped short. "Oooop, dear, I hope you have your house key. I forgot mine." Yoko didn't answer but used her key to call the elevator. John looked sheepishly at me. "I needn't have asked," he grinned.

Within the apartment, John guided me through a hall covered with photographs to the kitchen, where he instructed me to wait while he freshened up. Yoko was off in a different part of the apartment. As I looked around the huge, freshly painted kitchen, stocked with containers of tea and coffee, spices and grains, I heard voices from a distant bedroom: a child's giggling and a father's mock scolding. "So, you rascal, why aren't you asleep? Ahh haa! Well, I would have kissed you goodnight even if you were sleeping, silly boy."

John came tripping back into the kitchen, wholly revitalized, and, while putting a pot of water on to boil, he explained that their child Sean wasn't used to his and Yoko's new schedule, working on the album all hours. Before this project, John had been home virtually all the time.

Yoko entered the kitchen, wearing a kimonolike robe, and John poured three cups of tea. "Well, shall we start?" he asked as he sat down.

I looked at the two of them, waiting intently, and began. "The word is out: John Lennon and Yoko Ono are back—"

John interrupted immediately, and laughingly nudged Yoko. "Oh, really?" he joked. "From where?"

I smiled and continued: "—in the studio, recording again for the first time since 1975, when they vanished from public view. What have you been doing?"

John turned playfully to Yoko. "Do you want to start, or should I start?" he asked.

"You should start," she replied firmly.

"I should? Really? Okay. . . ." John leaned back in his chair, his hands clasped tightly around the cup of tea. He watched the steam float upward as he began.

LENNON: I've been baking bread.

PLAYBOY: Bread?

LENNON: And looking after the baby.

PLAYBOY: With what secret projects going on in the basement?

LENNON: Are you *kidding?* There were no secret projects going on in the basement. Because bread and babies, as every housewife knows, is a full-time job. There ain't no space for other projects.

After I had made the loaves, I felt like I had conquered something. But as I watched the bread being eaten, I thought, Well, Jesus! Don't I get a gold record or knighted or nothing?

And it is such a tremendous responsibility to see that the baby has the right amount of food and doesn't overeat and gets the right amount of sleep. If I, as housemother, had not put him to sleep and made sure that he was in the bath by 7:30, no one else would have. It's a tremendous responsibility. Now I understand the frustration of those women because of all the work. And there is no gold watch at the end of the day. . . .

PLAYBOY: What about the little rewards—the pleasure of watching somebody eat the bread or the baby sleep?

LENNON: There *is* great satisfaction. I took a Polaroid of my first loaf. [*Yoko laughs.*] I was overjoyed! I was *that* excited by it. I couldn't believe it! It was like an album coming out of the oven. The instantness of it was great. I was so into it, so thrilled with it, that I ended up cooking for the staff! Every day I was cooking lunch for the drivers, office boys, anybody who was working with us. "Come on up!" I loved it.

But then it was beginning to wear me out, you see. I thought, What *is* this? Screw this for a lark. I'd make two loaves on Friday and they'd be gone by Saturday afternoon. The thrill was wearing off and it became the routine again. So the joy is still there when I see Sean. He didn't come out of my belly but, *by God*, I made his bones, because I've attended to every meal, and to how he sleeps, and to the fact that he swims like a fish. That's because I took him to the "Y." I took him to the ocean. I'm so proud of those things. He is my biggest pride, you see.

PLAYBOY: Why did you become a househusband?

LENNON: It was a case of heal thyself.

ONO: It was asking, "What is more important in our life?"

LENNON: It was more important to face ourselves and face that reality than to continue a life of rock 'n' roll show biz, going up and down with the winds of either your own performance or the public's opinion of you. And it was something else, too. Let's use Picasso as an example. He just repeated himself into his grave. It's not to take away from his great talent, but his last forty years were a repetition. It didn't go anywhere. What do you call that? Living on your laurels.

You see, I found myself in my midthirties in a position where, for whatever reason, I had always considered myself an artist or musician or poet or whatever you want to call it and the so-called pain of the artist was always paid for by the freedom of the artist. And the idea of being a rock 'n' roll musician sort of suited my talents and mentality, and the freedom *was* great.

But then I found I wasn't free. I'd got boxed in. It wasn't just because of my contract, but the contract was a physical manifestation of being in prison. And with that I might as well have gone to a nine-to-five job as to carry on the way I was carrying on. Rock 'n' roll was not fun anymore. So there were the standard options in my business: going to Vegas and singing your greatest hits—if you're lucky—or going to hell, which is where Elvis went.

ONO: You can become a stereotype of yourself. We may have been heading that way. That is one thing we did not want to be. This is what I really despise about the art world. You get a tiny idea like, "All right, I'm an artist who draws circles." You stick to that and it becomes your label. You get a gallery and patrons and all that. And that's your life. And next year, perhaps you'll do triangles or something. There's such a poverty of ideas. Then if you go on and continue doing that for maybe ten years or something, people realize you are someone who continued ten years and you might get a prize. [*Chuckling*] It's such a ridiculous sort of routine.

LENNON: You get the *big* prize when you get cancer and you've been drawing circles or triangles for twenty years.

ONO: And then you die.

LENNON: Right. The biggest prize is when you die—a really big one for dying in public. Okay: Those are the things we are *not* interested in doing.

[*John clutched a spoon as he spoke, tapping it lightly on the table, keeping a beat that his words seemed to follow.*]

That's why we ended up doing things like bed-ins, and Yoko ended up doing things like pop music. With our first attempts at being together and producing things together, whether they were bed-ins or posters or films, we crossed over into each other's fields, like people do from country music to pop. We did it from avant-garde left field to rock 'n' roll left field. We tried to find a ground that was interesting to both of us. And we both got excited and stimulated by each other's experiences.

The things we did together were all variations on a theme, really. We wanted to know what we could do together, because we wanted to be together. We want to work together. We don't just want to be together on weekends. We want to be together and live together and work together.

So the first attempts were the bed-ins. We attempted to make music together, but that was a long time ago. People still had this idea the Beatles were some kind of thing that shouldn't step outside of its circle, and it was hard for us to work together then. We think either people have forgotten or they have grown up. Now we'll make the foray into the place where she and I are together and it's not some wondrous mystic prince from the rock world dabbling with this strange Oriental woman, which is the picture projected by the press before.

PLAYBOY: After all that, why now?

LENNON: Well, the spirit moved me. Yoko's spirit never left her. But my spirit moved me to write suddenly, which I haven't done for a long, long time. Also, I had been concentrating on being a househusband and I had sort of half-consciously wanted to spend the first five years of Sean's life actually giving him all the time I possibly could.

ONO [*to John*]: I think that it's not that the spirit moved you. [*To me*] I think that while he was sort of doing his thing about tuning in to Sean and tuning in to family and all that, or *because* of those things, his spirit rejuvenated. He did that instead of just dishing out records as he used to.

LENNON: Yeah, you're right. I was trying to say that. Maybe I didn't say it clearly. I *could* have continued being a craftsman, but I am not interested in being a craftsman, although I respect craftsmen and all the rest. I wasn't interested in proving I could go on dishing things out every six months like—

PLAYBOY: Like Paul [McCartney]?

LENNON: Not only Paul. Like everybody. So the experience of being a full-time parent gave me the spirit again. I didn't realize it was happening. But then I stepped back for a moment and said, "What has been going on? Here we are: I'm going to be forty, Sean's going to be five. Isn't it *great!* We survived!"

I am going to be forty, and life begins at forty, so they promise. Oh, I *believe* it, too. Because I feel fine. I'm, like, *excited.* It's like twenty-one—you know, hitting twenty-one. It's like: *Wow!* What's going to happen next?

2

The room had grown chilly. John popped up to close the window, which had been opened slightly. He turned his chair around before sitting again. He leaned it back and gently rocked as we continued.

LENNON: Suddenly it all came through to me like, *pow,* in the form of songs, although it all must have been on my mind somewhere or other all these years.

ONO: Yes, these songs are really inspired songs.

LENNON: There isn't one where I had to sit down and sort of *try* to make a dovetail joint.

PLAYBOY: Had it gotten to that uninspired point before?

LENNON: Yes, quite often.

PLAYBOY: On your and Yoko's albums?

LENNON: I think I was more in a morass mentally than Yoko was. If you listen to *Walls and Bridges* [Lennon's last album] you hear somebody that is depressed. You can say, "Well, it was because of years of fighting deportation and this problem and that problem,'' but whatever it was, it sounds depressing. The guy knows how to make tables, but there's no spirit in the tables.

I'm not knocking the record. But I'm saying it showed where I was. It's a reflection of the time, where I was—

ONO: It was a last breath—

LENNON: It was a depression—

ONO: It *was* a breath, though, a real breath.

LENNON: It was like *phewwww* [*exhaling*]. It doesn't make it more or less, but that's what it is.

PLAYBOY: How did you decide on the next step—rather than trying for another last breath?

LENNON: Well, walking away *is* much harder than carrying on. I know; I've done both. I hadn't stopped from '62 till '73—on demand, on schedule, continuously. And walking away *was* hard. What it seemed like to me was, This must be what guys go through at sixty-five when suddenly they're not supposed to exist anymore and they are sent out of the office. I thought, Well, oughtn't I? Shouldn't I? Shouldn't I be, like, going to the office or *something?* Producing *something?* Because I don't exist if my name isn't in the papers or if I don't have a record out or on the charts, or whatever—if I'm not seen at the right clubs. It must be like the guys at sixty-five when somebody comes up and goes [*knocks on the long, oak kitchen table: knock, knock, knock*], ''Your life is over. Time for golf.''

PLAYBOY: But your retirement was self-imposed?

LENNON: Self-imposed, yes, but still the feeling is there. Suddenly there's a whole big space that seems to be unfillable. And naturally it got filled because that's the law of the universe: Leave a space and something will fill it.

PLAYBOY: Most people would have continued to churn out the product. Why were you able to see a way out?

LENNON: Most people don't live with Yoko Ono.

PLAYBOY: Which means?

LENNON: Most people don't have a companion who will tell the truth and refuse to live with a bullshit artist, which I am pretty good at. I can bullshit myself and everybody around. Yoko: That's my answer.

PLAYBOY: What did she show you?

LENNON: She showed me the *possibility* of the alternative. "You don't *have* to do this." "I don't? Really? But—but—but—but . . ." Of course it wasn't that simple and it didn't sink in overnight. It took constant reinforcement.

ONO: It all shows how contaminated our minds are by society. We were taught and educated to achieve things or be something and, of course, doing something in the house is achieving something, but people don't recognize that. When John and I would go out, people would come up and say, "John, what are you doing?" They wouldn't believe he could simply—in quotes—be a househusband. But at least they asked him; they never asked me, because, as a woman, I wasn't *supposed* to be doing anything.

PLAYBOY: What were you doing then, Yoko?

LENNON: When I was cleaning the cat shit and feeding Sean, she was sitting in rooms full of smoke with men in three-piece suits that they couldn't button.

ONO [*speaking softly, precisely*]: I handled the business: old business—Apple, Maclen [the Beatles' record company and publishing company, respectively]—and new investments.

LENNON: We had to face the business. It was either another case of asking some daddy to come solve our business or having one of us do it. These lawyers were getting a quarter of a million dollars a year to sit around a table and eat salmon at the Plaza—I don't know if I can get sued for this—but most of them don't seem really interested in solving the problems. Every lawyer had a lawyer. Each Beatle had four or five people working for him. So we felt we had to look after that side of the business and get rid of it and deal with it before we could start dealing with our own life. And the only one of us that has the talent or the ability to deal with it on that level is Yoko.

ONO: We had to clean up. There was a demand about dealing with the business that needed to be filled. "Business" isn't such a terrible word. For us, "business" is something practical to our needs.

PLAYBOY: Yoko, did you have experience handling business matters of this proportion?

ONO: I learned. The law is not a mystery to me anymore. Politicians are not a mystery to me anymore. At first my own accountant and my own lawyer could not deal with the fact that I was telling them what to do.

LENNON: There was a bit of an attitude that this is John's wife, but surely she can't *really* be representing him.

ONO: Even now, there are many lawyers who write a letter and circulate it to all the directors of the corporation. I'm one of the directors, but instead of sending it to me, they send it to John or to *my* lawyer. You'd be surprised how much insult I took from them initially. There was all this "But you don't know anything about law! I can't talk to you." I said, "All right, talk to me in a way that I can understand it. I am a director, too."

LENNON: They can't stand it. But they *have* to stand it, because it is she who represents us. [*Chuckles*] They're all male, you know, just big and fat, vodka lunch, shouting males, like trained dogs, trained to attack all the time.

We made it fun, too, like [*to Yoko*] when you went to the meeting with the ten Jewish lawyers wearing an Arab headdress that we brought back from the pyramids.

ONO [*laughing*]: Everybody was just *looking*.

LENNON: Recently she made them about five million dollars and they fought and fought not to let her do it because it was her idea and she is a woman and she's not a professional. But she did it, and then one of the guys said to her, "Well, Lennon does it again." But Lennon didn't have anything to do with it.

ONO: I wouldn't say anything. I said, "Thank you," and hung up. I've learned; I'm being mellow. There is all this talk about the record we are working on now:

about John's album with a song or two sung by Yoko. I'm leaving it alone. You know why? Because my businesswoman instinct tells me that it is better for the deal.

LENNON: We've learned to come in sort of gently. We can't come smashing in like, "Hi! It's John and Yoko naked in bed with flags and Yoko screaming and him playing wild guitar in the back." We're just coming in through the back door.

ONO: In the old days I used to think, Well, I have a good song and I should be on the "A" side of a single, but these days I'm sort of wiser.

LENNON: I keep telling her "B" sides don't get played. I want her on the "A" side. Anyway, Jack [Douglas] and I will talk her into having a single. "Every Man Has a Woman" is a bloody good single. I am all for hit records. I don't care if she's leading or not.

ONO: Anyway, the relationship is better because both of us have experienced another side—John in the house, me in the office.

LENNON: It saved my life.

PLAYBOY: Meaning?

LENNON: I was stuck in the feeling that one did not—was not justified in being alive unless one was fulfilling other people's dreams, whether they were contractual dreams or the public's dreams, or fulfilling my own dreams and illusions about what I thought I was *supposed* to be, which, in retrospect, turned out to not be what I am.

PLAYBOY: Which Yoko showed you.

LENNON: And thank goodness. A lot of artists kill themselves because of it, you know, whether it be through drink, like a Dylan Thomas; or through insanity, like a Van Gogh; or VD and craziness, like a Gauguin, painting a picture for his child which he never spent any time with. He was trying to create a masterpiece for the child, and meanwhile the child died, and anyway Gauguin got VD and the masterpiece burned down. Even had it survived, better he should have stayed with the kid. That was the conclusion I came to.

Before, I sensed all this, I suppose, but I couldn't see a way out. And that's the bit about two heads are better than one. "Where two are gathered together . . ." to quote Bob Dylan's favorite attorney.

Yoko laughed and rolled up her eyes. "Yeah," she said, "but do we have to bring Bob Dylan into this?"

"Edit!" said John, slicing the air with an imaginary editor's knife.

The telephone had been suspiciously quiet all evening, but the buzzer inevitably sounded as John began to speak. Yoko yawned wearily as she answered it. When she hung up, she stood to leave. "I tell you what," she said. "I'm very tired. You give him some more and I'll join you in a bit."

"We'll go till half nine," John responded, "because it's better when the two of us are here. It sparks off, you know. So we'll go on a while."

Yoko quietly left the room, and John rose to get the pot of hot water to refill our cups of tea.

LENNON: So finally I saw it. I thought, My God! I exist independently of that.
PLAYBOY: Which must have been really—
LENNON: Mind-blowing. It was—
PLAYBOY: And invigorating—
LENNON: It was more than that. It was rediscovery of the self! It was like repossession of your own self, reclaiming myself.

[John reached for a cigarette—a Gauloise, as usual—and offered one to me. I shook my head. "That's right, no nicotine for you," he said. He put the cigarette in his mouth and fumbled through his pockets. "She pinched my lighter," he complained, shaking his head and chuckling. "It always happens." He stood up, turned on a burner on the gas range, and bent over to

light the cigarette. He turned off the gas, stretched, and sat down again, letting out a big cloud of smoke.]

PLAYBOY: Why is it so special for you and Yoko?
LENNON: Well, you're asking why we met. I mean, I don't know. It's like asking why were you born. I can give you theories of karmic pasts and things like that, but I've no idea why. But why it continues is because we want it to continue and work to continue.

There seem to be certain cycles that relationships go through. The critical points are at different parts of the different cycles. The new way of talking is like, ''Well, why work on a relationship? We just stop and get another one.'' But the karmic joke is, presuming you're lucky enough to find a new relationship anywhere near the relationship you're giving up—or exchanging, or walking away from, or destroying by inattention or inadvertence or selfishness or whatever it is—that you have to go through it over and over and over again right up until you're seventy.

People never grasp the fact that they're going to have to go through the same thing again. They get to the sort of five-year stretch or the seven-year itch or whatever these tension points are that seem to be organic, built in, like the tide coming in and going out. It's like every time the tide goes out you quit—you move your house or something. I'm not making it clear here, but you get where I'm going. . . .

PLAYBOY: Yes, yes, but what made you *see* that?
LENNON: When she kicked me out, I saw I was kicked out. When I was kicked out, I realized where I was, which was on a raft in the middle of the universe, and whatever happened, presuming I could have started another relationship, I would have ended up in the same place—*if I was lucky*. And that's a big *if*.

PLAYBOY: You're speaking about your separation in the early Seventies.
LENNON: Seventy-three, or whenever we were sepa-

rated, which is sort of a very cold way of saying it. It took a while, but that's what I saw. If I was lucky . . .

It's like what they say about karma. If you don't get it right in this lifetime, you have to come back and go through it again. Well, those laws that are sort of cosmically talked about, accepted or not but talked about, apply down to the most minute detail of life, too. It's like "Instant Karma," which is my way of saying it, right? It's not just some big cosmic thing, although it's that as well, but it's also the small things, like your life here and your relationship with the person you want to live with and be with. There are laws governing that relationship, too. You can either give up halfway up the hill and say, "I don't want to climb the mountain, it's too tough, I'm going to go back to the bottom and start again," or you can do it this time.

PLAYBOY: But you once decided it was too tough.

LENNON: I did. But I didn't see any of this then. Yoko and I were lucky enough to go through that and come back and pick up where we left off, although it took us some kind of effort and energy to—to blend in again and get in the same sync again. It took some time.

PLAYBOY: Was your decision to become a househusband a result of the separation as well?

LENNON: I could say yes and then it would be a pat thing: "Oh, they did this because of this. . . ." But it's not true at all. There's just more to it than that. But you could say, or I could say—'cause she might say a different thing entirely and it would still be true—"Yes, right, we got back together and we decided that this was our life, that having a baby was important to us and that everything else was subsidiary to that, and therefore everything else had to be abandoned." That abandonment gave us the fulfillment we were looking for and the space to breathe and think and reestablish our dreams. As she said in one of her songs a long time ago, which was a quote from one of her books which was even twenty years earlier than that, "A dream you dream together . . ." or "A dream you dream alone is . . ." I don't know, you'll have to look it up. "A dream you dream alone is one thing, a dream you dream together is reality." So we reestablished our dream together.

We both laughed. The actual quote turned out to be, "A dream you dream alone is only a dream. A dream you dream together is reality."

3

With that, the cassette popped up. We continued talking for hours past the 9:30 deadline and John was still excited and inspired. When another tape popped up around midnight, he said: "Put the tape on one more time and we'll have another cup and then call it a night."

PLAYBOY: I'm curious why you're doing this interview in the first place.

LENNON: To communicate and, frankly, to expose . . . We might be famous to certain people, but some people don't know about John and Yoko, believe it or not. And we need exposure. We don't need publicity, but we need to explain what we're doing.

PLAYBOY: I know a great deal of concern and interest is genuine. I'm sure it's occasionally oppressive, but people out there really care about what you're up to.

LENNON: Yes, and it's nice to talk. I mean, we haven't communicated outside for a long time and we're gonna enjoy it and have fun with it. I mean, I'm enjoying this.

PLAYBOY: Will you follow the release of the new record with a tour?

LENNON: Well, we probably will, you know. I wouldn't have believed it a month ago. But then I thought, What the hell, why not? If it's enjoyable and if it doesn't become something that one doesn't want to do, 'cause it's nice to get up and sing sometimes, like it's nice to make music. I don't want to get mixed up in deals and business and spin-offs and pressures, though, because I don't need *that* anymore. Once was enough. But sure, I'd like to get up on stage with Yoko and a good band and play these songs [*laughs*] and really *do* 'em, because the band's hot as shit. They just come off the album and they were all good—we've got the good feeling among ourselves. So it would be great. I'm just a little nervous about all that goes on around it. But I think we can probably handle it a bit better this time. . . .

PLAYBOY: On your terms.

LENNON: Right. That's it, do it on our terms, and therefore to enjoy it. Because if we don't enjoy it, the audience doesn't enjoy it. We did have fun doing a lot of the shows in the late Sixties and Seventies. We did all sorts of live performances. I think we must have done about twenty concerts in all . . . of different descriptions, from her concert at Cambridge in '68 and me just being on the feedback guitar, to Madison Square Garden or Live Peace in Toronto with an unrehearsed rock 'n' roll band behind us just giggin'. I mean, we had fun on all those gigs. I don't see why we couldn't have fun again, and sing *these* songs. But if you said this two months ago, I'd have said, "Are you *kidding?*"

PLAYBOY: The album will end with the chant we heard today, "One World . . ."

LENNON: ". . . One People."

PLAYBOY: Another kind of—

LENNON: Subliminal message, right [*laughing*].

PLAYBOY: Is that when hard times will be over—when we become one world, one people?

LENNON: No, no, no. We're one world, one people whether we like it or not. Aren't we? I mean, we can *pretend* we're divided into races and countries and we can carry on pretending that until we stop doin' it. But the reality is that it is one world and it is one people.

PLAYBOY: The step after "Imagine". . .

LENNON: That's the way it is *really*. "Imagine" said, "Well, can ya *possibly imagine* it?" "Consider *this!*"

PLAYBOY: And now that you've considered it . . .

LENNON: Now that you've considered it . . .

PLAYBOY: Open your eyes.

LENNON: [*excitedly*]: Yeah, right! Right! But I don't want it to come across like: "I am . . ." or "We are the awakened spirit. You are the sheep that will be shown the way. . . ." It's not that. And that is the danger in saying anything, you know.

PLAYBOY: Especially for you, because people are looking . . .

LENNON [*excitedly*]: Yeah, right! Right! But I don't leaders, watch yer parking meters. . . . [*Chuckling*] We'll get into that, but you know, leaders is what we *don't* need. We can have figureheads and we can have people that we admire and like to have standing up and all that. We can have examples. . . . But leaders is what we *don't* need. It's the utopian bit again. We're all members of the conceptual utopia. So let's not go round and round it: It's one world, one people, and it's a statement as well as a wish. [*Laughing softly*] So welcome to the dress rehearsal of *Double Fantasy*.

PLAYBOY [*referring to the day's recording session*]: At a dress rehearsal you get a little extra of the—the energy of creation. I'm sure the feeling of today's session, for instance, will be passed on through the record, but there's nothing like the experience itself.

LENNON: You know, Yoko was overwhelmed. I was overwhelmed, but I'm a guy. . . . You saw that she was actually overwhelmed. She started to cry at the session, you know. Then she must have sort of contained it and released it later when she cried again. Females just have the ability to let it come right through. I *felt* that way, but didn't allow myself—I'm not going to consciously cry in front of the engineer and the guy from PLAYBOY and all that. . . . But I felt like just sort of getting on my knees and saying, "Hallelujah!" or something, which probably would have been fine, too. But I thought, Well, ya have to keep an ear open—you know, all that rationalization. [*laughing*] "Important, serious work to be done here—can't be cryin' and feeling things. Gotta get on with the music." [*Smiling serenely*] But it was rather a good day, wasn't it?

PLAYBOY: It was a *great* day.

LENNON: It was great, can't *believe* it.

Once again the recorder clicked off, signaling another tape's end. "Guess that means it's time to quit," John said. The apartment was silent as I packed up my notes and micro cassette and standard tape recorders. John laughed about it. "All you beautiful boys with all your little toys," John sang, quoting Yoko's song. "She's got us down pat, huh?" John walked me to the elevator and I bid him goodnight. "It was a good, full day. So I'll see you in the A.M., huh?" he said as the elevator door closed.

The old, creaking elevator descended slowly. I left the Dakota and wished the night guard a good evening. Outside I waited for a taxi on the relatively silent New York street.

4

Yoko's office, where I arrived the following morning at 10:00 sharp, was an unusual sight. After waiting in the outer office filled with desks, a wall of files whose headings ranged from "Holsteins" to "Palm Beach," and the Lennons' album covers and a collection of photographs decorating the walls, I removed my shoes before treading on the deep white carpet of the inner sanctuary. Cut-glass cases that held strange Egyptian artifacts, such as a gray skull and a baby's breastplate of gold, were artfully lit in shadows of the many green plants. All was under a ceiling painted in blues and whites: billowing clouds reflected in angled mirrors surrounded by molded gold. At one end of the office hung a portrait of John and Sean, both with shoulder-length hair, painted early that summer in the Bahamas. Beneath the portrait was a piano. An ivory and jade inlaid oak box rested on a glass coffee table cased in black iron. A gold snake slithered along a crossbar below it. A huge, plushy white couch and matching chair formed an "L" around the table. The chair was Yoko's; from it she conducts the Lennons' business, and from there she greeted me.

John sleepily dragged into the office, signaled hello, and plopped onto the floor cross-legged. We talked about the album; Yoko had given me the lyrics the day before. After a second cup of coffee, I returned to a subject begun the night before.

PLAYBOY: Your split-up was very public. How much of what was printed was accurate?

LENNON: As much as is accurate in general in the media. A pinch of truth and a lot of herbal dressing.

ONO: It was accurate that we were separated; but when two people are separated, they automatically assume the guy left the girl and the poor girl is suffering and in tears, and when he comes back, she's so glad he came back. One thing that really upset me was that—you see, both of us sort of talked about the separation and said, "Let's do it." It wasn't like either of us was suffering about it. We felt we needed the space to think. . . .

LENNON: Well, *I* suffered—

ONO: Okay, but—

LENNON: We talked about it and she kicked me out is what actually happened.

PLAYBOY: Why?

ONO: Well, I think I really needed some space because I was used to being an artist and free and all that, and when I got together with John, because we're always in the public eye, I lost the freedom. And also, both of us were together all the time—

LENNON: Twenty-four hours a day—

ONO: Twenty-four hours a day. And the pressure was particularly strong on me because of being the one who stole John Lennon from the public or something.

LENNON: Right! First she supposedly split the Beatles up, and then she's the one stoppin' them from getting back together. It's mommy's fault. *That* bit!

ONO: Whatever the reason is, I was under very strong pressure and I think my artwork suffered. I suffered a lot and so I thought I wanted to be free from all that. I needed the space to think. So I thought it would be a good idea that he would go to L.A. and just leave me alone for a while.

PLAYBOY: What a horrible place to send somebody. What happened, John?

LENNON: Well, first I thought, Whoopee! Bachelor life! Whoopee, whoopee! And then I woke up one day and thought, What is this? I want to go home. But she wouldn't let me come home. That's why it was eighteen months instead of six. We were talking all the time on the phone and I kept saying, "I don't like this. I'm out of control. I'm drinking. I'm getting into trouble and I'd like to come home, please." And she's saying, "You're not ready to come home." "What are you saying?" Well, okay, back to the bottle . . .

PLAYBOY: Yoko, what did that mean—you're not ready?

ONO: I don't know, I mean . . .

LENNON: She has her ways, whether they be mystical or practical. When she says it's not ready, it ain't ready.

PLAYBOY: Back to the bottle?

LENNON: Yeah, I was just insane. The lost weekend

that lasted eighteen months. I've never drunk so much in my life, and I've been drinking since I was fifteen. But I really tried to drown myself in the bottle, and it took an awful lot. I don't seem strong physically that much, but it just seems to take an amazing lot to put me *down*. And I was with the heaviest drinkers in the industry, which is Harry Nilsson and Bobby Keyes and Keith Moon and all of them, and we couldn't pull ourselves out. I think Harry might be still trying, poor bugger—God bless you, Harry, wherever you are—but Jesus, I had to get away from that, because somebody was going to die. Keith Moon did. It was like who is going to die first? Unfortunately Keith was the one. But I got out.

PLAYBOY: It was all because of being apart?

LENNON: Yeah. I couldn't stand it. I absolutely couldn't stand it.

PLAYBOY: And Keith and Harry and the others had their own reasons for being miserable?

LENNON: Yeah. It was "Let's all drown ourselves together." I don't know whether they would agree with that; but looking at it from where I was sitting, it looked like that. "Let's kill ourselves but do it like Errol Flynn"—you know, the macho way. It's embarrassing for me to think about the period, because I made a big fool of myself.

PLAYBOY: That must have been the time the papers came out with reports about Lennon running around town with a Tampax on his head.

LENNON: Everything got so exaggerated. All the Tampax story was that we were in a restaurant drinking, not eating, as usual at those gatherings, and I just happened to go to the gents to take a pee. There was a brand-new, fresh—not Tampax but Kotex—just on the toilet. And you know that old trick where you put a penny on your forehead and it sticks? I was just a little high—it was still early, you see—and I just saw the thing, picked it up, and slapped it on my forehead [*acting it out as he speaks*] and it stayed. So for a gag I walked back from the toilet. It's like the old Beatle stories: There was a lot of drinking and carousing when we were in Germany, but the stories built out of all proportion over the years. There was a lot of heavy boys' fun, but nothing like the stories you hear if you go to Hamburg now. So the Kotex thing was a bit like that. I walked back from the toilet, sat down at the seat, and everybody went "Ha ha ha," and I left it on until it fell off and that's all.

ONO: I heard about it and thought, What's wrong with that?

LENNON: Like, so he had a Kotex on his head, big deal.

ONO: That reminds me, by the way, when we were dating a long, long time ago and I was making little objects and all that, I sent John a box of Kotex. It was a piece that you open a box of Kotex and there are a lot of Kotex pads in it and inside there is a red broken cup, called a "mend piece." You know, you're supposed to mend the cup that is broken. And the idea is that when you open the Kotex box and you go through it, there is something red in there, and I think he was rather embarrassed. [*To John*] Don't you [*laughing slyly*]?

LENNON: Only because I was married at the time and my wife wondered who this woman was that sent me a box of Kotex. [*Much laughter*] You know, I didn't know much about her work then. I met her and we were sort of dating on the side and . . . I didn't know what to do about it. "Well, this is actually an artist's work, my dear, and there's nothing to it. It's just—she happens to work with Kotex. One of the avant-garde fields, Kotex, you see." Her mother was around—the ex-wife's mother, you know—and they're all *looking*. There's a box of Kotex coming from this woman who I'm supposedly having a platonic relationship with, which it *was* at the time.

ONO: Yes, it was.

LENNON: So Kotex has been a big thing in our lives.

ONO: So anyway, from this end I'm reading about

these things and thinking, He's still John, doing it in that style. He wasn't hurting anybody. A lot of it was rather funny, wasn't it?

LENNON: Thank you, dear. She was the only one that didn't put me down for that period because (a) she knew I was suffering horribly, and (b) she said, "What's *wrong* with having a Kotex on your head?"

They're all going on about whether I shouted too loud in a restaurant or had a Kotex on my head, which is harmless drunk fun. . . . When I called her, she said, "That was a good event." I was calling saying, "Gee, I'm in big trouble. They're all talking about the Kotex and I shouted at a concert" and she's saying, "So what? You never hurt anybody." I thought, Okay, okay, she doesn't mind it. I'm not going to give a damn whether the reporter in *Rolling Stone* likes it or not. She made me feel all right about it, although it's still embarrassing to think that I've been out of control in-public.

I was like that as a kid, you know. At art school. If you go to my art school and ask about my career there, it was mainly being drunk. When you get old and famous, it takes on different connotations. I was thinking, Why are they attacking me? They're always talking about the good old days when Flynn and the old boys were hard drinkers tearing up the town: those *real men*. When it's today and it's the rock 'n' rollers, it's "How *dare* they?" It reminds me of my auntie, who loved to read about Oscar Wilde and Van Gogh—artists—in books, but no bizarre people around the house.

PLAYBOY: Speaking about those times, what about the Smothers Brothers episode?

LENNON: Oh, yes—well, there was this resurrection of the Smothers Brothers going on at a club in L.A. and Harry and I were drunk. I was drinking brandy alexanders for the first time—that was Harry's drink; they taste like milkshakes, and I was knocking them back as if they were—and suddenly I was in the fourth dimension. In the fourth dimension I noticed what I'd always secretly thought, that Dickie Smothers was an asshole even though I always liked Tommy. And so that's what I said, but because I was drunk, I said it out loud. I was a born heckler.

PLAYBOY: Especially after a batch of brandy alexanders.

LENNON: On brandy alexanders I'm a very loud heckler. So I yelled, "Dickie, you're an asshole." Tommy tried to cover it up. I don't know, what bothered me was that the Bring-Back-the-Smothers-Brothers thing is part of the Bring-Back-the-Beatles and Dig-up-John-Kennedy things. People want Ted Kennedy to be John Kennedy and the people who used to be the Beatles to be the Beatles. Although I regret hurting anybody's feelings, I still feel that way about the act. I always thought Dickie was a wimp and Tommy was all right. Maybe I shouldn't have said it out loud. Who cares?

So then somebody said something to me and I shouted sarcastically, "Don't you know who I am?" They were throwing me out. I was messing around, you know. I was hysterically drunk. And of course I was being encouraged by Harry.

If I died—they way Dylan Thomas died—they'd be saying, "What a wonderful, colorful way to go." Because I'm alive, it's not so wonderful. It was the worst time of my life.

ONO [*looking thoughtfully at John*]: In those eighteen months, we *were* very good friends, weren't we? I mean . . .

LENNON [*to Yoko*]: Well, you stopped me from going right over the edge, you know. [*To me*] There was hardly a week passed that we wouldn't talk. She was supporting me, saying, "Just look after your health" and things. I'd say, "I waaaanna come home." "Not yet."

PLAYBOY: This was '73 and '74?

LENNON: I don't know. But my life's documented by when albums came out. We were working on the *Rock 'n' Roll* album and *Walls and Bridges* and Harry's album, and there was Phil Spector running away with the tapes and Harry Nilsson and lots of drinking craziness. And then I sober up and I bring the tapes back to New York because I want to get home to Yoko and I also want to get the tapes and I want to get myself out of L.A. and out of the bottle. I come home and she still won't let me home, so I'm sort of hanging around New York for a bit and I keep calling, "Can I come home yet?" "You're not ready." "*I'm* ready." "No, you're not ready."

PLAYBOY: Yoko, why *did* you kick John out?

ONO: There were many things. I'm what I call a "moving on" girl; there's a song on our new album about it. Rather than deal with problems in relationships, I've always moved on. That's why I'm one of the very few sort of survivors as a woman, you know. Women tend to be more into men usually, but I wasn't. . . .

LENNON: Yoko looks upon men as assistants.

ONO: Yeah. [*Laughs*] It's me, okay. . . .

LENNON: Of varying degrees of intimacy, but basically assistants. And *this* one's going to take a pee. [*He exits.*]

ONO: I have no comment on that. But when I met John, women to him were basically people around who were serving him. He had to open himself up and face me—and I had to see what he was going through. But . . . I thought I had to "move on" again because I was suffering being with John. I thought I wanted to be free from being Mrs. Lennon.

PLAYBOY: There's something that doesn't jibe. You said that part of the problem was that you were together too much—twenty-four hours a day. But you are together twenty-four hours a day *now*.

ONO: I have to clarify that. It's a very strange thing that society can do that much to a relationship, but it does because we're social animals. We're social beings. A relationship is not isolated from society. [*John reenters the room.*] Suppose a guy was married to a very famous girl—I'm sure the same thing would happen. It's a very hard position.

LENNON: If the situation were reversed, I'd be Mr. Ono.

ONO: And you'd be so humiliated you'd want to leave. Not because you don't love her but because you feel like, I can't stand this situation because it's a situation where you're castrated. Society doesn't understand that women can be castrated. I felt castrated. Before that I was doing all right, thank you. My work might not have been selling much, I might have been poorer—whatever. But I had my human pride intact and I was doing all right. The most humiliating thing was to be looked at as a parasite—a being that's fed. "All right, you don't have to worry about money. . . ." That sounds silly, but it's more than that. A man would feel inadequate, or whatever, in that position, but somehow society thinks that if you're a woman it's all right.

LENNON: One Beatle assistant, who shall remain nameless, in the upper echelon of Beatle assistants, leaned over to Yoko in the early days when we were doing a lot of stuff together—there was a John and Yoko office in Apple and we would hold long, mad press conferences to announce our whatevers: We're all gonna wear bags, or whatever—and he leaned over and said, "You know, you don't have to work, you've got enough money, now that you're Mrs. Lennon. . . ." That was in '68 or something. In those days I would say, "Oh, don't worry about that. . . ." But by the time we got to '73, you know, a good few years of that kind of attitude emasculates you. Is that the word?

ONO: Exactly. I was emasculated.

LENNON: And on top of that, me being me is enough without the pandemonium . . .

ONO: You see, I always was more macho than most guys, in the sense that whenever I had a situation where I was married or something like that, I was the breadwinner. I wouldn't want to stay at home and take care of the child or something. I was always doing that. So suddenly I'm with somebody who I can't possibly compete with on the level of earnings. So what am I going to do? My pride was being hurt all the time. Early on, when John was a Beatle, we stayed in a room and John and I were in bed and the door was closed and all that, but not locked, and one of the Beatle assistants just walked in and talked to him as if I weren't there.

LENNON: He was used to people being in bed with me, so any female was just sort of nobody.

ONO: It was mind-blowing. I was invisible.

LENNON: And when she complained to me about it, I couldn't understand. "He's good old Charley," or whatever. "He's been with us twenty years. . . ." "She'll come around."

The same kind of thing happened in the studio. She would say to an engineer, "I'd like a little more bass or a little more treble" or "There's too much of whatever you're putting on," and they'd look at me and say, "What did *you* say, John?" Those days I didn't even notice it myself. Now I know what she's talking about. In Japan, when I ask for a cup of tea in Japanese, they look at Yoko and ask, "He wants a cup of tea?" in Japanese.

PLAYBOY: Knowing Yoko, I can't imagine she took it very well.

LENNON: No, she fought every inch of the way.

ONO: Until finally I couldn't take it any longer. I would have had the same difficulty, though, even if I hadn't gotten involved with ah . . .

LENNON: John. John's the name.

ONO: With John. But John wasn't just John, he was also his group and the people around them. When I say John, it's not just John—

LENNON: That's John. J-O-H-N. From Johan, I believe.

PLAYBOY: So you made him leave?

ONO: Yes.

LENNON: She don't suffer fools gladly, even if she's married to him. So anyway, we allowed ourselves to be so affected by outside influences and pressures that we just *burst*. That's what it was. The pressure was too much, so we burst.

ONO: Society can break an individual. That is what happened.

5

The buzzer sounded. The car had arrived to take us to the studio. On the way out, a young girl accosted John with "When are you going back with the Beatles?" John snapped, "When are you going back to high school?"

The day's session—Yoko singing lead vocals to "Kiss Kiss Kiss"—ended early. Back at the apartment, we continued.

PLAYBOY: How did you finally get back together?

ONO: Well, all these people from the West Coast had been calling and saying, "Listen, you'd better come over here because he's really a mess over it . . ." and I'd say, "Well, he's just having fun" and all that. The business people think, Well, this is John Lennon, a valuable item—you'd better take care of it.

LENNON: Yes, I'm property. Not a sex object but a something object.

ONO: And I'm someone to take care of it. That's all it is to them—his wife, so come take care of him. But I have very complex feelings, too. I don't operate like that—"Come get him." But I heard that he was doing an Elton John concert in New York and I went to that—which was a very strange thing for me to do.

PLAYBOY: At Madison Square Garden?

ONO: Yes. So I went there and I was watching him

from the audience and everybody was applauding like crazy—the house *shook* when he came on—and he was there bowing, but that's not what I saw. Somehow he looked very lonely to me and I began crying. Somebody next to me asked, "Why are you crying?" "I'm not crying," I remember saying. But somehow it hit me that he was a very lonely person up on stage there. And he needed me. It was like my soul suddenly saw his soul. So I went backstage. I said hello and he said hello.

LENNON: We have a photograph of the moment we met—looking a bit coy and shy. A photographer just happened to catch it. I couldn't have gone on if I had known she was in the audience. It was hard enough. I went on because I had promised Elton I'd do it. He sang on a single that turned out to be a cut from *Walls and Bridges*, "Whatever Gets You Through the Night." He sang harmony on it and he really did a damn good job. So I sort of halfheartedly promised that if "Whatever Gets You Through the Night" became number one, which I had no reason to expect, I'd do Madison Square Garden with him. So one day Elton called and said, "Remember when you promised . . ." It wasn't like I promised some agent or something, so I was suddenly stuck. I had to go on stage in the middle of nothing.

And then there she was [*smiling*].

PLAYBOY: What happened next?

ONO [*laughing*]: We dated. We laughed about it then, too. It was really like starting to know each other again. I wasn't sure yet. I was thinking, Am I going to go back to that—um—pandemonium?

LENNON: The madhouse . . .

ONO: So I wasn't sure, you know.

LENNON: 'Cause letting me back in is more than just—you get more than me, right? She had to make the choice whether it was worth lettin' me back in, not just me but with this mythology that comes with me.

ONO: So I was thinking, Am I going to get into this

again just because I saw his soul or something? So there was some hesitation. Some moments when we really felt, Ah, we'd be crazy *not* to be together, I would think about it all and finally say, "All right, you'd better go now." One time I came back from a show and somebody told me John was here. They said, "Well, we put him in the living room, is that okay?" So I went to the living room and he was there and we said hello and all that and then we sort of cried on each other's shoulders and while we were doing that going on inside me was, Okay, crying's fine, but this means the whole pandemonium again. So okay, well, goodbye. . . . But we were *crying* about it. It was very difficult.

LENNON: It'll make a great movie. [*Laughs*] So then we realized that there was a lot of—as we call it   holes in our aura, space that had to be gently healed between us.

ONO: We had to clean our aura.

LENNON: We had to clean the . . . separation period from us. We had to sort of wash it off somehow, and that was a delicate operation—almost as delicate as first meeting and that getting-to-know-each-other business.

PLAYBOY: What had changed to allow things to work?

ONO: Well, it slowly started to dawn on me that John was not the trouble at all. John was a fine person. It was society that had become too much. I'm thankful to John's intelligence—

LENNON: Now, get that, editors—you got that word?

ONO [*laughing*]: —that he was intelligent enough to know that this was the only way that we could save our marriage, not because we didn't love each other but because it was too much for me. Nothing would have changed if I had come back as Mrs. Lennon again.

PLAYBOY: What did change?

ONO: It was good for me to do the business and regain my pride about what I can do. And it was good to know what he needed, the role reversal; that was so good for him.

LENNON: We learned that it's better for the family if we are both working for the family, she doing the business and me playing mother and wife. We reordered our priorities. The number-one priority is her and the family. Everything else revolves around that.

ONO: It's a hard realization. These days the society prefers single people. The encouragements are to divorce or separate or be single or gay—whatever. Corporations want singles—they work harder if they don't have family ties; they don't have to give too much to the family; they don't have to worry about being home in the evenings or on weekends. By freeing people from the family life, they are pulling people right into the capitalist trap. For capitalism to accelerate, it's better for everybody to be single. There's not much room for emotions about family or personal relationships.

LENNON: There's another reason: Everybody has to buy their own TV, their own phone, their own apartment, their own clothes. You know, there's no sharing or anything.

ONO: Choosing careers over family life may seem fine, but by choosing career, people are also choosing the corporation. Their heart is not anywhere but with the company. The more devoted workers are promoted. They're really turning into more efficient components.

We have basic human feelings, right? The body. Women have the womb. But to compete, we deny those feelings. A woman has to deny what she has, her womb, if she wants to make it. It's a deception: the Madison Avenue slick woman as the "free" woman. "Free" means we were becoming whores. We're taking the pill and sticking Tampax in and making it very convenient for the guys. Then we realized taking pills gives us cancer. Tampons give us cancer. We're *looking good* but we're *dying*.

LENNON: You've come a long way, baby.

ONO: That's part of the new woman. It seems only the privileged classes can have families. Nowadays, maybe it's only the McCartneys and the Lennons or something.

LENNON: Everybody else becomes a worker-consumer.

ONO: And then Big Brother will decide—I hate to use the term "Big Brother"—

LENNON: Too late. He's got it on tape. [*Laughs*]

ONO: But finally the system—

LENNON: Big Sister—wait till *she* comes!

ONO: The system will decide, "Okay, some of you will go into the division of creating babies."

LENNON: There'll be test tubes and incubators. Then it's Aldous Huxley.

ONO: No, no, wait a minute. We don't have to go that way. Some of us can awaken to the fact that we don't have to deny our organs—

LENNON: Some of my best friends are organs—

ONO: The new album—

LENNON: You brought it around to the album, very good—

ONO: —The album fights these things. The messages are sort of old-fashioned: family, relationships, children.

LENNON: Right. We're talking about ordinary things. Usually when you get a male and a female on a record, they're saying, "I love you," right? That's the basic thing. But it's not a dialogue between a man and a woman like Ike and Tina Turner did it.

ONO: It's more that something has happened between us and here it is. Sometimes the relationship goes up and sometimes down. . . .

LENNON: It's very honest. It's not a sex fantasy, as a lot of the stories in the press are saying. [*Mocking*] "They're putting their sex fantasies down on a record! Ohmigosh!" Yeah, I've read that. I read everything. That's like when we did the bed-ins. They all came charging through the door thinking we were going to be screwing in bed. And of course we were just sitting there with peace signs.

PLAYBOY: The album is a dialogue between the two of you. How autobiographical is it?

LENNON: If you ask me that next year, I might have a different answer, but now I'll say that it is completely autobiographical. It's about us over the last five or six years. It's like a movie, though, and the script is constantly changing. When you shuffle a scene here and there, does it change the story? I don't know. So there is a thread there that is a story, but we've shuffled the scenes. And whether it is complete or not—well, it's like "Who shot J.R.?" Get the next album and see. It's like *Apocalypse Now*! There are two or three endings. I'm not sure how it ends. We've got the idea that it starts like this, then there's the scene where he says this and she says that and sometimes they talk together, which means sometimes we sing together. . . .

ONO: But it's also not just showing what happened, but what we gained from the experiences. It reflects the kinds of things we learned from life, you see.

LENNON: Right. Rather than it being a diary, it's sort of like after you've written a diary, you look back and ask, "What did I gain from it all?" It's reflections on notes already taken.

It is, of course, artistic, and therefore cannot be taken verbatim. We used actual situations to write songs. "Losing You" is apparently about our separation, but it was actually written when Sean and I were in Bermuda and I couldn't get through to her.

She was in New York and was coming in for the weekend. We were like, "Mummy's coming! Mummy's coming!" You know, it's the role reversal, like "Daddy's coming, daddy's coming!" as if daddy were abroad to Germany or something—only instead of daddy going away and the family staying home, the family went away and daddy stayed home, 'cause daddy/mommy was in the office. So we were, "She's coming! She's coming for the weekend!"

So we were thrilled to see her, but she was on the phone the whole time she was with us. We heard her on the phone selling this cow, and I was joking about it 'cause I didn't know what was going on. It was only later that I found out what it was. Only Yoko could sell a cow for a quarter of a million. . . .

So she went back home, and I was trying to call her but I couldn't get through! After that weekend, I was so frustrated and I couldn't get through! And I wrote the whole thing about that, but I was half thinking about the real separation. The direct feeling was of not being able to reach her, of not being able to get through, that she was slipping away. It drove me crackers—just long enough to write a song.

PLAYBOY: It's odd relating a song to its creation. Are you conscious of the feelings your songs communicate?

ONO: Pop songs are a very strong form of communication. Most people think you write a pop song because it is a very commercial form and you can make more money for it. That's not it at all. Pop music is the people's form, you see. Intellectuals trying to communicate with the people usually fail. It's like trying to communicate in archaic German or French in Japan. If you go to Japan, talk Japanese. Forget all the intellectual garbage, all the ritual of that, and get down to the real feeling—simple, good human feeling—and express it in a sort of simple language that reaches people. No bullshit. If I want to communicate with people, I should use their language. Pop songs are that language. They're a very strong form of communication.

Another thing is that we are trying to be more and more aware of the healing power of sound. It's true that certain sounds will heal illness, heal all sorts of negative forces in the world. A pop song may be very short, but it is very powerful.

LENNON: So is a heartbeat.

ONO: That's right. Underneath the whole record is a heartbeat. Music circulates because of the vibration, and so you have to be very careful what you put out.

PLAYBOY: Then your purpose is to do more than entertain. The hope is that the record will be inspiring and will move people to feel or act differently—which is just what people want from you: some prescription for life. Is this more responsibility than you would choose to have?

LENNON [*emphatically*]: No. No, because it's the same bit about saying that the Beatles led the Sixties. It's not true. [*Faster and clearer, seemingly a rhythmic chant*] The idea of leadership is a false god. If you want to use the Beatles or John and Yoko or whoever, people are expecting them to do something *for* them. That's not what's going to happen. But they are the ones who didn't understand any message that came before anyway. And they are the ones that will follow Hitler or follow Reverend Moon or whoever. Following is not what it's about, but leaving messages of "This is what's happening to us. Hey, what's happening to you?"

We're sending postcards and letters. That's what we do. And that's different. Do you see?

PLAYBOY: But do you think most people take it as it's intended?

LENNON: I don't know. When you cook a meal, you cook it and people eat it and you can tell by the expression on their faces what they think of it. I have a hopeful wish/prayer that they will take it in the spirit that it is given, which is with love and a lot of sweat, the life experience of two people.

PLAYBOY: But your postcards *do* have a message—everything from "God" to "Imagine" to the songs on *Double Fantasy*.

ONO: Let me explain it this way. People think of fantasy as different from reality, but fantasy is almost like the reality that will come. Everyone creates the fantasies, so everyone creates the reality. If you look at it that way, then George Orwell will create *1984*. That's the general trend of the male species, I think—creating that kind of fantasy.

[*John coughed loudly and then chuckled. "He coughs, bracket," using his fingers to draw imaginary brackets in the air like the ones that contain such asides in* PLAYBOY. *Yoko didn't miss a beat.*]

ONO: Like H. G. Wells. People say, "Incredible! What he said is happening!" But actually it is not a prophecy but a form of prayer making it happen.

LENNON: I agree with that. That's what she's been telling me for years, since we met. What do they call it? Wish fulfillment. The other day I saw an article. [*To Yoko*] Remember? I showed you. This guy had predicted the Third World War and what world events would lead to it. Now they're all saying, "Oh, look, it's happening just like he said!" Our game, or whatever it is, has always been the same. While that kind of article is actually a commercial for war, eventually creating war, we were doing commercials for peace.

When we did the bed-ins, we told the reporters that and they responded, "Uh-huh, yeah, sure. . . ." But it didn't matter what the reporters said, because our commercial went out nonetheless. It was just like another TV commercial. Everybody puts them down but everybody knows them, listens to them, buys the products. We're doing the same thing. We're putting the word "peace" on the front page of the paper next to all the words about war.

PLAYBOY: With hopes that wishful thinking will create a new reality?

LENNON: That's it. You got it.

PLAYBOY: Which explains Yoko's song "Hard Times Are Over." I had a hard time understanding it. Hard times are far from over. But *say* that hard times are over and they *will* be?

LENNON: Exactly.

ONO: But also notice I'm saying, "Hard times are over *for a while*." I could simply say, "Hard times are over." But it's a very delicate thing. It's like weaving, which goes in and out slowly. You must do it slowly. Saying "Hard times are over for a while" is sort of a delicate way of wishing. It's not like saying, "I want to live forever. Make sure I live forever." It's not that sort of arrogance. It might happen, but there is a strong repercussion. So I want to be more delicate, to ride the wave which is yin/yang, breathing in and out. It's not like I'm wishing for something arrogant. It is fair and it can happen.

LENNON: It's the same idea we had for "Give Peace a Chance." It wasn't like "You *have* to have peace!" Just give it a *chance*. We ain't giving any gospel here—just saying how about *this* version for a change? We think the future is made in your mind.

ONO: I think it's not so much *we,* if you meant the two of us, but *all* of us are part of the future. The future is already within us. I think that the world is going around and is alive because some people really know that whatever they think really happens. It isn't on an esoteric, intellectual level, but I really believe that whatever you think will happen. So we're sort of responsible for our thoughts, even. We all have very negative thoughts and all that, too, and I'm not saying we should repress them, but somehow *transform* them into something positive.

PLAYBOY: If John and Yoko came out with an album predicting the apocalypse—

LENNON: I don't think we'd put it out. We'd be digging trenches and preparing rice. [*Turning serious*] The apocalypse is not necessarily so. *It ain't necessarily so,* as they used to say.

ONO [*smiling and shaking her head*]: I don't know why people always project things negative, though you shouldn't be afraid of projecting something negative as long as there is the other side, too. We all do have some garbage in us and we shouldn't be afraid of bringing it out, as long as we end with a positive period. We have some songs on the album that can be considered negative, but at the same time the fact that we can honestly state those feelings is very positive, and we get a certain atonement through that. There is a negative side, so let it out, sing it, and dispense with it. Singing a negative song does not mean we are setting up a negative fantasy. Instead, we are using the negative to get to the positive.

*Earlier, John had been talking about "Losing You,"
explaining that he retitled the song "(Afraid I'm) Losing You" because of a fear that the unqualified title
could work as a self-fulfilled prophecy.*

6

PLAYBOY: So where do all the negative, violent fantasies come from?

LENNON: All the science-fiction writers and movie-
makers have generally been male, projecting crisis after
crisis—World War III up in the sky with space suits on.
That message, the male message, is the one that is
communicated.

PLAYBOY: Why do you think the male message is
consistently violent?

ONO: There might be biological reasons males project
that violent image because we—

LENNON [*letting out a weary sigh*]: Come on, give
us a break—

ONO: —because we have the womb and you must
have the womb-envy thing.

PLAYBOY: As opposed to penis envy?

ONO: Well, that's another thing. You ask *any* woman.
No woman ever went through penis envy. We never
did. The books say we're supposed to, but look who
wrote the books. We never had penis envy. But men do
have womb envy, because we are directly connected to
life and we give life—

PLAYBOY: And men traditionally make war and take
away life.

ONO: Yes, but the tradition can easily be changed
once you are aware of it.

LENNON: The female message has not been heard or listened to for centuries and it's only starting to come out. Although there is a thing called the "women's movement," it's like society took a laxative and just farted. They haven't really had a good shit yet. It really hasn't started. The seed was planted sometime in the Sixties, but the real changes are slow to come down.

ONO: It's a matter of changing your consciousness. When John first read *The First Sex* by Elizabeth B. Davis, he was up until late at night and he started crying. I think he really felt that tremendous guilt that the male species has about what it allowed women to go through. Then in these past five or six years, he consciously did the role reversal and went through a very new experience, which inspired him to write the type of songs as the ones on the album.

On the other hand, I was one of those women who really didn't understand men, and through him, through John, I realized a lot about the male struggle in the world. I learned that men suffer, too. He learned about women's suffering. The social structure causes a great deal of the suffering. The only way to change it is by being aware of it. It sounds simple. It is simple. Most important things are simple, like breathing. You know how to do it. Just by changing your consciousness. We don't even have to do it very much.

There is great danger in the way we're going. Part of the reason things have developed this way has to do with the division of labor. It was established a long, long time ago—it was more convenient for men to go out and cut trees while the women were nursing the children. That started the whole cycle of men hunting and the so-called hunting instinct, which we have too, by the way. The division of labor caused the problem. So women's voice became a voiceless voice. Men believed in verbalizing things. Men believed in mediums such as writing. Women did go into writing as well, but they believed more in a sort of psychic means of communication. Now they're trying to do things the way men do, which is a pretty dangerous way. It's a healthy change in the sense that they're not just sitting in a rut, that we are trying, exploring new fields. In that sense, it's inspiring and it's healthy, but there are dangers—that we become men, *we* become the macho society.

LENNON: I know that comparison is odious, and comparisons with the so-called black movement are even more odious, but this is a little like the first black awakening. First, there was a tendency to imitate whitey and straighten the hair and things like that. And suddenly they thought, What the hell are we doing? We have to be ourselves. We are beautiful in ourselves, though there's still a little of the straighten-the-hair business. It's not a put-down. It's a natural evolution.

And the same comparison again—which I don't like to do but I have to now that we're doing it—is that sort of racist remark, "Well [*in a deep put-on voice*], we've given the blacks education and freedom to vote, how come they're not all equal now? There's something wrong with their genes!" [*Normally but passionately*] Garbage! That trick! That trick! It's like their brain ain't developed. That's simply lack of use of muscle, either brain muscle or physical muscle. The same as the women's bodies aren't developed to do hard labor because they simply weren't developed.

ONO: But I think this is wrong—I don't think we should try to develop our muscles—

LENNON: No, I don't mean physically—

ONO: Yeah, but even on a brain level. For instance, we always debate, Shall we send Sean to school or not? I don't suppose there's any reason to send him to school, because he should pick up language, he should pick up writing and all that, when he wants to. In fact, children who stay without the knowledge of writing for a long time become more psychic. So there is that, too. . . .

LENNON: *Remain* more psychic . . .

ONO: Oh, right, remain. *Remain* more psychic. Exactly. So from that point of view the fact that women are not verbal, or this way or that way or whatever women are *not* that men *are,* I think our way of thinking and our way of feeling is really helping the world.

LENNON: How about *saving* the world?

ONO: Saving the world. Right. So it's a pity to change that.

LENNON: But once the change gets out of the crawling stage, there will be a dialogue. The result will be [that] men's intuition or psychicness or whatever word you want to use, which we lost, will be redeveloped. Women's other potentials will be developed, and we will share the burden equally according to each individual's—what's the word?

ONO: Ability.

LENNON: Right. And each individual leading instead of always delegating that a black person does this and a child does that. . . .

PLAYBOY: John, does it take actually reversing roles with women to *really* understand?

LENNON: It did for this man. I can't talk for men per se, although I can generalize about it. For me, it took a commitment to make the change.

PLAYBOY: Inspired by books like *The First Sex*?

LENNON: Yes, through reading. And through living with the Ono here. She doesn't let anything slip by.

But deciding to make the change was like deciding "I am going to be a musician" or something. I was always musical, but there was a point when I said, "I am going to learn this instrument. I really want to get into this through this door." So the opportunity was presented to me not just through Yoko but through having a child and through being in the specific situation I was in when I started this, which was after years of fighting with immigration and lawsuits and all these things until there was almost no alternative but to go through this door—and going through the door changed me permanently.

So that's what it was. There are many, many reasons why things happen, but there are a couple of good ones right there.

PLAYBOY: How have things gone for you since you made that decision?

LENNON: There are ups and downs like with anyone, but we know what is most important: being together. As she says, "Where two are gathered together . . ."

ONO: When two are gathered together there is nothing you can't do. As a power it is very strong.

PLAYBOY: It's very inspiring, but what about the people without that kind of love and companionship—all the lonely people?

LENNON [*seriously*]: Go and get it.

ONO: Yes.

PLAYBOY: It's as simple as that?

LENNON: "Go and get it" is a flip way of saying that if you will be open to the possibility, you—

ONO: —will receive it.

PLAYBOY: Do you agree that having it makes all the difference in the world?

LENNON: Absolutely. It's the difference between life and death.

ONO: And on a practical level, the power of two people praying, wishing, whatever, is strong.

LENNON: The consciousness is, "Let's see what we shall pray for together. Let's make it stronger by picturing the same image, projecting the same image. And that is the secret. That is the secret. Because you can be together but projecting different things.

ONO: Double fantasies.

LENNON: Double fantasies at the same time. And you get whoever's fantasy is strongest at the time or you get nothing but mishmash. You're defeated both ways.

ONO: Of course he has different dreams and I have different dreams, too. And that's a weakness. In other words, when you say two people want the same thing, that doesn't happen *all* the time. So when it happens, it's really powerful. Sometimes two people might be praying but at the same time one could be thinking about something else. Then it doesn't happen. That sort of unified wishing or praying doesn't happen that simply. We go many ways but finally come together and wish that everything is going to be all right.

7

PLAYBOY: After finding such contentment and happiness in your new roles *away* from the public, why are you returning to public life?

LENNON: You breathe in and you breathe out. We breathed in after breathing out for a long time. The *I Ching* calls it sitting still. A lot more can happen when you're not doing anything than when you appear to be doing something. Although it looks that what John and Yoko were doing for five years was not doing anything, we were doing a hell of a lot. Sitting still is one way of describing it. Sitting still, amazing things happen, you see. And now we're not sitting still. Now we're moving around. And maybe in a few years we'll sit still again. Because life is long, I presume.

So now we are breathing out. One must do both: One withdraws, one expands; tide in, tide out. It's better to breathe in and breathe out rather than just always trying to breathe out. You can run out of breath. Also, we feel like doing it and we have something to say, as we've talked about.

PLAYBOY: And it was Yoko who caused or allowed you to be able to breathe in?

LENNON: And the fact that I was smart enough to catch on. I mean, I *saw* when the possibility was offered to me.

PLAYBOY: But hadn't you accomplished that when you left the Beatles?

LENNON: Well, that was a *similar* experience, yes. I was too scared to break away from the Beatles, but I'd been looking to it since '65 when we stopped touring. And maybe Paul had been, too—I don't know. I can't speak for the others.

But, um, I made a movie—*How I Won the War* with Dick Lester—which never got seen much but did me a lot of good. Well, it did me a lot of good to get away, and it *was* a withdrawal. I was in Almería, Spain. I wrote "Strawberry Fields" there, by the way. I was there for six weeks and it gave me time to think and to be separate from the others but still be working and not be left in the house alone. And I used to be there and think, like a lot of people do, Well, what can I do if I don't do that?

And so from '65 on I was sort of vaguely looking for somewhere to go, but I didn't have the nerve to really step in the boat by myself and push the boat off. So I sort of hung around, and when I met and then fell in love, well, it was *"My God! This is different from anything before. This is something other. I don't know what it is, but this is* fine.*"* [*Chuckling, looking skyward*] *Thank you, thank you, thank you!* It's *more* than a hit record. It's *more* than gold, it's *more* than everything. *It's more than. This is something indescribable.*

That's what happened. We just got so self-involved. So I did free myself physically from the Beatles, but not mentally. Mentally I was still carrying them around in the back, back, back of my head, although the initial love blinds all: Everything is under shining lights and you want everybody to be happy just like you. It's rather dizzying. Later on, love is different and one can slow down a little. It's not less, just different. And so therefore I could lift out all this garbage that was still being carried 'round which was influencing the way I thought and the way I lived and all the rest of it. And then finally free myself from the mental, let's call it, mental Beatles or Sixties or whatever it was. So the first one was a physical escape. The second was a mental escape.

PLAYBOY: But you *had* left, apparently completely, since *Plastic Ono*.

LENNON: Yes, but still I was carrying the Beatles around like a lot of other people are carrying the Beatles around—"When are they coming back?" and "What do you think of Paul?" You know, I *don't* think . . .

PLAYBOY: On our way to the studio today, you responded to the girl who asked you "What do you think of Paul?" with a "When are you going back to high school?"

LENNON: Well, it's the same thing, you know. That old gang of mine. That's all over. When I met Yoko is when you meet your first woman and you leave the guys at the bar and you don't go play football anymore and you don't go play snooker and billiards. Maybe some guys like to do it every Friday night or something and continue that relationship with the boys, but once I found *the* woman, the boys became of no interest whatsoever, other than they were like old friends. You know: "Hi, how are you? How's *your* wife?" That kind of thing. You know the song: "Those wedding bells are breaking up that old gang of mine." Well, it didn't hit me till whatever age I was when I met Yoko, which was twenty-six. Nineteen sixty-six we met, but the full impact didn't . . . we didn't get married till '68, was it? It all blends into one bleeding *movie!*

But whatever, that was *it*. The old gang of mine was over the moment I met her. I didn't consciously know it at the time, but that's what was going on. As soon as I met her, that was the end of the boys, but it so happened that the boys were well known and weren't just the local guys at the bar. These were guys everybody else knew. But it was the same thing—but everybody got so *upset* about it and *angry!* Only Yoko and I were so involved with each other we just went and made the records and did bed-ins and somehow blasted our way through it. But there was a lot of shit thrown at us, a lot of painful stuff.

PLAYBOY: From the outside, it appeared that all the talk wasn't affecting you.

LENNON: Of *course* it affected us. We're both sensitive people and we were both hurt by a lot of it. And we couldn't *understand* at first. We just couldn't understand it. I mean, if somebody starts saying, "Why are you with that ugly woman?" or something, you say, "What do you *mean?* I am with this goddess of love and the fulfillment of my whole life! Why are you saying this? Why does somebody want to punish me for being in love with her?"

PLAYBOY: Why does somebody want to throw a rock at your glass bubble?

LENNON: YESSSSS! *Why would they want to do that?* Our love survived it, but it was pretty violent. I mean it was pretty nasty, a lot of it, and we almost went under. But we managed to survive and here we are, and we're thankful. [*Skyward again*] *Thank you, thank you, thank you!* And it was a long haul and I don't want to go back at all. Thankfully we're still here. There was also a lot of love thrown our way and a lot of prayer, or whatever you call it. And that also helped us survive.

PLAYBOY: But what about the charge that John Lennon is under Yoko's spell, under her control?

LENNON: Well, that's rubbish, you know. Nobody controls me. I'm uncontrollable. The only one that controls me is me, and that's just barely possible.

PLAYBOY: Still, many people believe it.

LENNON: Listen, if somebody's gonna impress me, whether it be a Maharishi or a Yoko Ono, there comes a point when the emperor has no clothes. There comes a point where I will *see*. So for all you folks out there who think that I'm having the wool pulled over my eyes—well, that's an insult to me. Not that you think less of Yoko, because that's *your* problem; what I think of her is what counts! But if you think you know me or you have some part of me because of the music I've made, and then you think I'm being controlled like a dog on a leash because I do things with her, then screw you. Because—fuck you brother and sister, you don't know what's happening. I'm not here for you. I'm here for me and her and the baby!

ONO: Of course it's a total insult to *me*—

LENNON: Well, you're always insulted, my dear wife. It's natural—

ONO: Why should I bother to control anybody?

LENNON: She doesn't need me—

ONO: I have my own life, you know—

LENNON: She doesn't need a Beatle. Who needs a Beatle?

ONO: Do people think I'm that much of a con? John lasted two months with the Maharishi. Two months! I must be the biggest con in the world because I've been with him thirteen years.

LENNON: But people do say that.

PLAYBOY: That's my point. Why?

LENNON: They want to hold on to something they never had in the first place. Anybody who claims to have some interest in me as an individual artist, or even as part of the Beatles, has absolutely misunderstood everything I ever said if they can't see why I'm with Yoko. And if they can't see that, they don't see anything. They're just jacking off to—it could be anybody: Mick Jagger or somebody else. Let them go jack off to Mick Jagger, okay? I don't need it.

PLAYBOY: He'll appreciate that.

LENNON: I absolutely don't need it. Let them chase Wings. Just forget about me. If that's what you want, go after Paul or Mick. I ain't here for that. If that's not apparent in my past, I'm saying it in black and green, next to all the tits and asses on page 196. Go play with the other boys. Don't bother me. Go play with the Rolling Wings.

PLAYBOY: Do you—

LENNON: No, wait a minute. Let's stay with this a second; sometimes I can't let go of it, like you can't sometimes. [*He is on his feet, climbing up the refrigerator.*] Nobody ever said *anything* about Paul having a spell on me, or me having one on Paul! They never thought *that* was abnormal—and in *those* days. Two guys together or four guys together! Why didn't they ever say, "How come those guys don't split up? I mean, what's going *on* backstage? *What is this Paul and John business?* How can they be together so long?" We spent more time together in the early days than John and Yoko: the four of us sleeping in the same room, practically in the same bed, in the same truck, living together night and day, eating, *shitting* and *pissing* together. All right? Doing *everything* together! Nobody said a damn thing about being under a spell. Maybe they said we were under the spell of Brian Epstein or George Martin [the Beatles' manager and producer, respectively]. There's always somebody that has to be doing something to you.

You know, they're congratulating the Stones on being together a hundred and twelve years. Whoopee! At least Charlie and Bill still got their families. In the Eighties they'll be asking, "Why are those guys still together? Can't they hack it on their own? Why do they have to be surrounded by a gang? Is the little leader scared somebody's gonna knife him in the back?" That's gonna be the question. That's a-gonna be the question. They're gonna look back at the Beatles and Stones and all those guys as relics. The days when those bands were just all men will be on the newsreels, you know: They will be showing pictures of the guy with lipstick wriggling his ass and the four guys with the evil black makeup on their eyes trying to look raunchy. That's gonna be the joke in the future, not a couple singing together or living and working together. It's all right when you're sixteen, seventeen, eighteen to have male companions and idols, okay? It's tribal and it's gang and it's fine. But when it continues and you're still doing it when you're forty, that means you're still sixteen in the head.

8

John ran out to ask an assistant to warm up the coffee and tea while Yoko and I chatted. When he returned, he continued, as if there had been no interruption: "The other point you are going to ask is, 'Why do it with Yoko?' or 'Why's she doing it with me?' "

I smiled. "No, I wasn't going to ask."

"But let's say they ask: 'Why do it together?' " he said. "Because together is the only way that it's fun."

PLAYBOY: It must be very liberating to have survived against all odds.

LENNON: Yeah, it's fantastic. So nothing to sweat about. Not to say that I have the answer and I never get nervous or paranoid about it, but I understand a lot more than I did then. And it seems okay to me.

[*Sighing*] Ahh, they call it life's experience, I suppose. I mean, lots of people have been through it before us. Every time everything seems new, because one goes through it, but people have been doing it for centuries. That was what I was going to say before when you said, "Well, a lot of people are waiting for this because of what you are going to say," or whatever. But (a) we've already said it, and (b) a hundred million other people have said it in the past, too. Anything we can say only reinforces what is in existence.

PLAYBOY: But perhaps you can say it in a way to get

through to somebody new, someone who hasn't gotten it no matter how many times it's been said.

LENNON: Yeah, and the way we say it is in today's language rather than in some archaic language. But nothing new under the sun, you know, nothing new to say. Only reinforcement of the same old message: The sun comes up and the sun goes down, it comes up again.

PLAYBOY: Besides the fans who are anticipating spiritual guidance or whatever, there is the record business anticipating your "product" as a cure for a suffering industry.

LENNON: It's a bit of a drag.

ONO: I don't think the whole recession in the music business exists. That again is a very male way of thinking. [*She and John exchange smiles.*] I think that if you look back at the Depression, people bought what they liked even then. The only reason the record world is going down is because they don't really have—

LENNON: The product. It's like the car industry. There is all this talk about the Germans and Japanese—the "other" is doing it to us.

Now we all were there in the early Seventies when the so-called Arab oil embargo caught us by surprise like the snow does every year in New York and the rain does every year in Los Angeles and the fog does every year in London and Liverpool: the big surprise that happens all the time. And they continued making old men's cars. Wishful fantasy fulfillment of the heads of the car companies who are all in their sixties and still designing cars from the Forties and Fifties—the big American car that everybody knew they didn't want. So everybody's buying Japanese and other foreign cars, not because they're unpatriotic, but because they're practical.

So now the car industry is trying to pass laws and it's pointing fingers and making commercials and the old men are coming out of their ivory towers saying, "Buy America" and "We're going to make the car you want."

Don't talk about it, man, just make the damn car, we'll buy it. You don't have to put an American flag on it. If it's good, we'll buy it. If it ain't no good, we're going to buy cars made in Venezuela.

In the Fifties, it was the British pointing their fingers at the Germans. It's simply that the Germans were making better products. Now it's the Japanese that are making better products, and. people are buying them. It's the same with pop music. The exec in the office goofed. They just have to give the product and people will buy it. You can't bewail the fact that you can't sell a tank to people who want to buy horses.

ONO: And the demand *is* there. People are dying to communicate, to be touched. But the record companies are doing a guessing game: "Maybe this will appeal to the public."

LENNON: You got computers trying to tell them what people want.

ONO: Exactly. That's not what we're doing. You asked us if the public will take this or not. Well, we're just giving part of our thing. If they take it or not, we don't know. It's not like it's a made-up thing that we think the public wants. It's our thing. If they're going to take it, they'll take it.

PLAYBOY: Do you have your own musical preferences these days?

LENNON: Well, I like all music depending on what time of day it is. I don't like styles of music or people per se. I can't say I enjoy the Pretenders, but I like their hit record. I enjoy the B-52s because I hear them doing Yoko. It's great. If Yoko ever goes back to her old sound, they'll be saying, "Yeah, she's copying the B-52s."

PLAYBOY: Do you listen to the radio?

LENNON: Muzak or classical. I don't purchase records. I do enjoy listening to things like Japanese folk music or Indian music. My tastes are very broad. When I was a housewife I just had Muzak on—background music—because it relaxes you.

PLAYBOY: Yoko?

ONO: No.

PLAYBOY: Do you go out and buy records?

ONO: Or read the newspaper or magazine or watch TV? No.

PLAYBOY: Another inevitable question: John, do you listen to your own records?

LENNON: *Least* of all my own.

PLAYBOY: Even your classics?

LENNON: Are you kidding? For pleasure I would *never* listen to them. When I hear them, I just think of the session—the forty-eight hours Paul and I sat up putting "the white album" [*The Beatles*] in order until we were going crazy; the eight hours of mixing "Revolution 9"—whatever. Jesus, we were sitting hours doing the bloody guitars. I remember every detail of the work.

PLAYBOY: Might you be overly critical of your old songs?

LENNON: I'm not critical. I just hear them and re-member the particular day. It's like an actor watching himself in an old movie. When I hear a song I remem-ber Abbey Road studio, the session, who fought with whom, where I was sitting, banging the tambourine in the corner . . .

ONO: In fact, we really don't enjoy listening to other people's work much. We sort of analyze everything we hear.

LENNON: Yeah, if it's bad we don't like it; if it's great we're angry that we didn't come up with it.

PLAYBOY: Yoko, were you a Beatles fan?

ONO: No. Now I notice the songs, of course. In a restaurant John will point out, "Ahh, they're playing George" or something.

PLAYBOY: Do you ever go out to hear music?

LENNON: No, I'm not interested. I might like Jerry Lee Lewis singing "Whole Lotta Shakin' " on the record, but I'm not interested in seeing him perform it.

PLAYBOY: Your songs are sung more than most other songwriters', John. How does that feel?

LENNON: I'm always proud and pleased when people do my songs. It gives me pleasure that they even attempt to do them, because a lot of my songs aren't that doable. I go to restaurants and the groups always play "Yesterday." Yoko and I even signed a guy's violin in Spain after he played us "Yesterday." He couldn't understand that I didn't write the song. But I guess he couldn't have gone from table to table playing "I Am the Walrus." [*Laughter*]

PLAYBOY: How does it feel to have influenced so many musicians?

LENNON: It wasn't really me or us. It was the times. It happened to me when I heard rock 'n' roll in the Fifties. I had no idea about doing music as a way of life until rock 'n' roll hit me.

PLAYBOY: Do you recall what specifically hit you?

LENNON: I think it was "Rock Around the Clock." I enjoyed Bill Haley, but I wasn't overwhelmed by him. It wasn't until "Heartbreak Hotel" that I really got into it.

I know Fats Domino was makin' records in '48, and there was lots of stuff called rhythm 'n' blues you could've called rock 'n' roll, but it was hard to get in England. Rock 'n' roll only came into our consciousness when white people did it. I think it was a euphemism for fucking—the actual expression meaning being in bed and rocking and rolling. So this bit about, "When did rock start?" really means "When did the honkies start noticing it?" "When did we know it was something strong and powerful and beautiful?" So it doesn't matter when; it's what it did to us that matters—that it changed *our* lives when we heard it.

PLAYBOY: What do you think of the direction music is going in now?

ONO: We were doing a lot of punk stuff a long time ago.

PLAYBOY: John and Yoko, the original punks.

ONO: You're right.

PLAYBOY: John, what's your opinion of the newer waves?

LENNON: I love all this punky stuff. It's pure. I'm not, however, crazy about the people that destroy themselves.

PLAYBOY: You disagree with Neil Young's lyric in "Rust Never Sleeps": "It's better to burn out than to fade away . . ."

LENNON: I hate it. It's better to fade away like an old soldier than to burn out. If he was talking about burning out like Sid Vicious, forget it. I don't appreciate the worship of dead Sid Vicious or of dead James Dean or dead John Wayne. It's the same thing. Making Sid Vicious a hero, Jim Morrison—it's garbage to me. I worship the people who survive. Gloria Swanson. Greta Garbo. They're saying John Wayne conquered cancer— he whipped it like a man. You know, I'm sorry that he died and all that—I'm sorry for his family—but he didn't whip cancer. It whipped him. I don't want Sean worshipping John Wayne or Johnny Rotten or Sid Vicious. What do they teach you? Nothing. Death. Sid Vicious died for what? So that we might rock? I mean, it's garbage, you know. If Neil Young admires that sentiment so much, why doesn't he do it? Because he sure as hell faded away and came back many times, like all of us. No thank you. I'll take the living and the healthy.

9

The following morning the three of us left the Dakota and walked the block and a half to La Fortuna, a neighborhood coffee shop on Columbus Avenue. Yoko and John ordered cappuccinos. John asked for a napoleon

*pastry. As we talked, he meticulously scraped the cream
from the center of the cake and licked it off his knife. He
ordered one more and did the same, again leaving the
light pastry. "Better than Oreos," he laughed.*

*A regular at the coffeehouse came by the table to say
hello. Yoko and John nodded politely as the gent dis-
coursed briefly on the harmonic passages within "Norwegian Wood." When the old man left with a wave,
John turned to me and said, "After all this time, I don't
have any idea what the fuck a harmonic is." As we
walked back to the Dakota, I broached John's favorite
subject.*

PLAYBOY: Do you mind talking more about Sean?
LENNON: I can talk about him forever.
PLAYBOY: Tell me a little about him.
LENNON: Well, you'll meet him soon enough. He's
special to us and he's beautiful physically and other-
wise. And that's the thing. . . .

We did send him to kindergarten once, but I realized
I sent him because I was getting tired. They're sending
the kids off earlier and earlier. I realize that most of the
school system and kindergartens are for the women or
the people who have to go out and work and cannot be
there. But this idea of sending the young people to one
prison and the old people to another prison when they're
a certain age—there's something *backward* about that.
[*Shaking his head*] The old people are there to look after
the young people. So if they take the old people out of
their prisons and the young people out of their prisons
and put them *together* somewhere, then we're going to
have some nice free children.

I think Sean's spirit is . . . he's traveled a lot, he's
with adults a lot. He goes wherever we go. He gets
plenty of child companionship as well, which everyone
says is so important—"Well, doesn't he need *children?*"
No, he'd sooner have his parents any day, as long as
we're around, though he doesn't have to be on my knee
all the time. Like all children, he likes to know that I'm

in the house, even if *he's* out. One big trauma for him was when he realized that sometimes *I* go out of the house, and then I come back.

One day I went out and came back in and he was kind of looking at me. "Well, where were you?" he said. I said, "Well, I just went out round the coffee shop. You know how *you* go out sometimes? That's what I did." That was a big moment for him, to realize that I exist outside the kitchen. It was amazing. They think when you're out of sight you vanish forever. They don't seem to grasp the idea that you will return. I mean, now he does. He's catching on. . . .

Outside the Dakota, John and Yoko signed a few autographs before we entered the lobby. We returned to Yoko's office. She was quickly briefed on business she had missed, and the three of us retreated to her office to continue.

PLAYBOY: Earlier you said that Sean is your biggest pride. Was he a planned child?

LENNON: Ahh, we worked *hard* for that child. We went through all hell together—through many miscarriages and terrible, *terrible* times. So this is what they call a love child in truth. We were told by doctors in England that we could never have a child. We had that sort of negative put on us. We'd almost given up: "Well, that's it, we can't have one then."

ONO: That was a challenge.

LENNON: That was a challenge. She was forty-three, so they said: "No way." They said she had too many miscarriages and when she was a young girl there were no pills so there are a lot of abortions and miscarriages and all sorts of things. [*Mockingly*] "Her stomach must look like Kew Gardens in London. It's a maze in there. . . ." The prognosis was "She's too old and you've abused yourself too much. You blew your jism by abusing your health as a rock 'n' roll patriot." There's something wrong with my sperm.

Well, what happened to us was a Chinese acupuncturist who's now dead, God rest his soul, in San Francisco, said, "Heck, you have a child. Just behave yourself. No drugs, no drink, eat well. You have a child in eighteen months." We said, "But the English doctors said I've abused myself in my youth and she . . . And there's no chance. . . ." "Forget what they said. Eat well and behave yourself. No drugs, no drink, eat well. You have a child in eighteen months." So we had Sean and I sent him a Polaroid of the baby just before he died. He died right after Sean was born.

You know, we were the positive thinkers and all that, but when this guy, this doctor, said we *couldn't* . . . well, that's when I realized that I did want a child and how badly. I wanted Yoko's baby, not *a* baby.

When Yoko became pregnant, we did the Sophia Loren bit for the nine months—you know, we took it very carefully because of both our histories. So it was nine months of sitting still, waiting for the baby. Not shaking around too much. We stopped smoking even before we conceived, and we were on a strict diet.

PLAYBOY: Were there any problems because of Yoko's age?

LENNON: Not because of her age, but because of a screw-up in the hospital and the fucking price of fame. Somebody had made a transfusion of the wrong blood type into Yoko. I was there when it happened, and she starts to go rigid, and then shake from the pain and trauma. I run up to this nurse and say, "Go get the doctor!" I'm holding on tight to Yoko while this guy gets to the hospital room. He walks in, hardly notices that Yoko is going through fucking *convulsions,* goes straight for me, smiles, shakes my hand, and says, "I've always wanted to meet you, Mr. Lennon, I always enjoyed your music." I start screaming: *"My wife's dying and you wanna talk about music!"* Christ! A miracle that everything was okay.

PLAYBOY: You said that you wanted a child, Yoko's

child, but had no prior interest in being a father. What changed?

LENNON: Well, both of us wanted to be a parent for the first time is what it was. Even though both of us had children by previous incarnations. We'd both been so self-occupied. It was also wanting a child that was *our* child as opposed to *a* child—'cause we could have adopted one, you know. Some people want *a* child, which I admire, too—people who have that generalized love. But we wanted *our* child.

PLAYBOY: A product of your love.

LENNON: Yes, a product of our love. It was also that we were finally unselfish enough to want to have a child. You know, 'cause we're really both selfish artists. We both have big egos and we're both completely involved in our work, so it was a kind of mutual awakening to want a child. It developed like that.

PLAYBOY: Was it the responsibility of a child?

LENNON [*thoughtfully and slowly*]: No, the *gift* of life. In the way we think, Sean chose us as parents. The gift of that responsibility doesn't end. I don't know if it ends when we die. It's an ongoing process. It's a tremendous gift and a tremendous responsibility. And I think responsibility was something I *never* wanted—of *any* description. Irresponsibility was what I craved. I couldn't face responsibility, I don't think. But facing it gave me the ability to *do* it, so that's the reward of facing something I was avoiding facing.

PLAYBOY: That was opposite everything you had geared your life on up to that time.

LENNON: Yes. It was a three-hundred-and-sixty-degree turnaround. And it was quite exciting. More than taking a tab of acid in 1965, you know, that kind of thing, which I thought was the biggest thing that ever hit the world at that time, you know. But this is *more than*.

PLAYBOY: You aren't sending Sean to school now, but what about later?

LENNON: Sean's not going to public school. We feel he can learn the three Rs when he wants to—or, I suppose, when the law says he has to; I'm not going to fight it. Otherwise, there's no reason for him to be learning to sit still. I can't see any reason for it. As I said, he now has plenty of child companionship, but he's also with adults a lot. He's adjusted to both.

I feel strongly about it. The reason why kids are crazy is that nobody can face the responsibility of bringing them up. Everybody is too scared to deal with children all the time, so we reject them and send them away and torture them. The ones that survive are the conformists—their bodies are cut to the size of the suits—the ones we label good. The ones that don't fit the suits are either put in mental homes or become artists.

PLAYBOY: Your son from your first marriage, Julian, must be in his teens. Have you seen him over the years?

LENNON: Well, Cyn got possession, or whatever you call it. I got rights to see him on his holidays and all that business and at least there's an open line still going. It's not the best relationship between father and son, but it is there. He's seventeen now. Julian and I will have a relationship in the future. Over the years he's been able to see through the Beatle image and to see through the image that his mother will have given him, subconsciously or consciously. He's interested in girls and autobikes now. I'm just sort of a figure in the sky, but he's obliged to communicate with me, even when he probably doesn't want to.

PLAYBOY: You're being very honest about your feelings toward him, to the point of saying that Sean is your first child. Are you concerned about hurting him?

LENNON: I'm not going to lie to Julian. Ninety percent of the people on this planet, especially in the West, were born out of a bottle of whiskey on a Saturday night, and there was no intent to have children. So ninety percent of us—that includes everybody—were accidents. I don't know anybody who was a planned child. All of us were Saturday-night specials. Julian is in the majority, along with me and everybody else.

Sean is a planned child, and therein lies the difference. I don't love Julian any less as a child. He's still my son, whether he came from a bottle of whiskey or because they didn't have pills in those days. He's here, he belongs to me, and he always will.

PLAYBOY: Yoko, your relationship with your daughter has been much rockier. The press covered your troubles extensively.

ONO: I lost Kyoko when she was about five. I was sort of an offbeat mother, but we had very good communication. I wasn't particularly taking care of her, but she was always with me—on stage or at gallery shows, whatever. When she was not even a year old, I took her on stage as an instrument—an uncontrollable instrument, you know. My communication with her was on the level of sharing conversation and doing things. She was closer to my ex-husband because of that.

PLAYBOY: What happened when she was five?

ONO: John and I got together and I separated from my ex-husband [Tony Cox]. He took Kyoko away. We tried to get her back.

LENNON: It was a classic case of men being macho. It turned into me and Allen Klein trying to dominate Tony Cox. Tony's attitude was "You got my wife but you won't get my child." In this battle, Yoko and the child were absolutely forgotten. I always feel bad about it. It became a case of the Shootout at the OK Corral: Cox fled to the hills and hid out, and the sheriff and I tracked him down. First, we won custody in court. Yoko didn't want to go to court, but the men—Klein and I—did it anyway.

ONO: Allen called up one day saying I won the court case. He gave me a piece of paper. I said, "What is this piece of paper? Is this what I won? I don't have my child."

I knew that taking them to court would frighten them, and of course it did frighten them. So Tony vanished. He was very strong, thinking that the capitalists with their money and lawyers and detectives were pursuing him. It made him stronger.

LENNON: We chased him all over the world. God knows where he went. *So if you're reading this, Tony, let's grow up about it. It's gone. We don't want to chase you anymore, because we've done enough damage.*

ONO: We also had private detectives chasing Kyoko, which I thought was a bad trip, too. One guy came to report, "It was great! We almost had them. We were just behind them in a car but they sped up and got away." I went hysterical. "What do you mean you almost *got* them? We are talking about *my child!*"

LENNON: It was like we were after an escaped convict.

PLAYBOY: Were you so persistent because you felt you were better for Kyoko?

LENNON: She got steamed into a guilt thing that if she wasn't attacking them with detectives and police and the FBI, then she wasn't a good mother looking for her baby. She kept saying, "Leave them alone, leave them alone," but they said you can't do that.

ONO: For me, it was like they just disappeared from my life. Part of me left with them. All I wanted was open communication with her. There was a time when John and I would be watching TV and there would be a child on and we would switch the dial because I couldn't bear seeing children. After some suffering, I think I have a sense of atonement about it. It probably was better for her to be with her father. But it wouldn't have hurt to have communication on the level I was hoping for.

PLAYBOY: How old is she now?

ONO: Seventeen, the same as John's son.

PLAYBOY: Perhaps when she gets older she'll seek you out.

ONO: She is totally frightened. There was a time where a meeting was set up between me and Tony. He wanted to see. But I was surrounded by Allen Klein and John and Allen's accountant and of course Tony got scared. Then there was a time in Spain when John and, again, a lawyer thought that we should kidnap her.

LENNON: Oh, no, it's all coming out. . . .

ONO: And we actually kidnapped her and went to court.

LENNON: I think I'll just go commit hara-kiri. . . .

ONO: In court they did a very sensible thing, taking her down in a room and saying, "Which one do you want to go with?" Of course she said Tony, she was so frightened the way we grabbed her and everything. So she went with Tony. So now she must be very scared that if she comes here she will never see her father again.

LENNON: She will have to be in her twenties to understand that we were idiots and we know we were idiots.

ONO: Maybe.

LENNON: She might give us a chance.

ONO: I probably would have lost Kyoko even if it wasn't for John. If I had separated from Tony, there would have been some difficulty.

LENNON: I'll just *half* kill myself then. . . .

ONO [*to John*]: Part of the reason things got so bad was because, with Kyoko, it was you and Tony dealing. *Men*. With Julian it was women—there was more understanding between me and Cyn.

PLAYBOY: Can you explain that?

ONO: For example, there was a birthday party that Kyoko had and we were both invited, but John felt uptight about it and he didn't go. He wouldn't deal with Tony. But we were both invited to Julian's party and we both went.

LENNON [*sighing*]: Oh, God, this too . . .

ONO: Or when I was invited to Tony's place alone, I couldn't go; but when John was invited to Cyn's, he did go.

LENNON: One rule for the men, one for the women.

ONO: So it was easier for Julian, because I was allowing it to happen.

LENNON: But I've said a million Hail Marys. What the hell else can I do?

PLAYBOY: Yoko, after this experience, how do you feel about leaving Sean's rearing to John?

ONO: I am very clear about my emotions in this area. I don't feel guilty. I am doing it in my own way. It may not be the same as other mothers, but I'm doing it the way I can do it. In general, mothers have a very strong resentment toward their children even though there's this whole adulation about motherhood and how mothers really think about their children and how they really love their children. I mean, they do, but it is not humanly possible to retain emotion that mothers are supposed to have within this society. Women are just too stretched out in different directions to retain that emotion. Too much is required of them. So I say to John—

LENNON: I *am* her favorite husband—

ONO: "—I am carrying the baby nine months and that is enough. You take care of it afterwards." It did sound like a crude remark, but I really believe that children belong to the society because we are all part of society, and society should have some system that would protect children. If a father raises the child and a mother carries it, the responsibility is shared. That is a better way. I am not criticizing myself. This is what I am, and I can't be anything else.

LENNON: She puts herself down as a mother, which is garbage.

ONO: No, I'm not putting it down.

LENNON: Well, there are "other" things you do which I can't do. He can wake you up in the middle of the night and you're right there for him. I'm like, "Oh, God, can't it wait till morning? . . ."

PLAYBOY: Did you resent having to take so much responsibility, John?

LENNON: Well, sometimes, you know, she'd come home and say, "I'm tired." I'd say, only partly tongue-in-cheek, "What the fuck do you think *I* am? *I'm* twenty-four hours with the baby! Do you think that's easy?'' I'd say, "You're going to take some more interest in the child!" I don't care whether it's a father or a mother. When I'm going on about pimples and bones and which TV shows to let him watch, I could say, "Listen, this is important! I don't want to hear about your twenty-million-dollar deal tonight!" It's hard to be on either side. Anyway, there should be support from society. [*To Yoko*] I would like both parents to take care of the children, but how is a different matter.

ONO: Okay, but now there are two conflicting messages coming to the mother: "Motherhood is beautiful," et cetera, but also there's this: "Too bad she's pregnant" and "She's just a housewife." And you have to be pregnant while at the same time you have to be a sex object. How much can you do? You have to have a beautiful figure *and* be pregnant.

PLAYBOY: You risk losing your husband as well because of changing from sex object to mother.

ONO: Exactly. And you even risk losing your apartment. I mean, some apartments don't let children in.

LENNON: It used to be dogs and Chinese. Now it's children and dogs, so we have come a long way.

ONO: Yeah, right.

LENNON: Dogs, Chinese, and Irish, I believe. It's hard to keep up.

ONO: We cannot be that image of a woman who is intelligent, beautiful, sexy, and achievement-oriented and be a housewife taking care of a child twenty-four hours a day. That's why I think it's unhealthy for mothers to have such a strong part in raising children.

PLAYBOY: And it's dangerous for the father to be so removed from raising children.

ONO: But I'll go a step further and say it's dangerous for a couple to have to be responsible for the child so much. The connection with the child is there anyway. I mean, it's my flesh and blood. So no matter where they go I have some connection. But it's almost like I did this beautiful painting or something and then someone tells me, "All right, you did this beautiful painting and now you have to maintain it: dust it and clean it and always look after it." That's the part that someone else can do and the child's better off for it and the parents are better off for it and the society is better off for it. Some people might say, "Oh, how horrible, what a mother!" but that way we can deal with a child better emotionally and physically. I mean a child has needs that I may not be the best to fulfill. There are certain things he or she would be better off getting from somebody else. So I said my piece about children. Society should take care of children.

LENNON: Well, I'll go as far as agreeing that there should be some fallback on society.

ONO: All right, we should compromise. The society should at least be more understanding.

LENNON: You should be able to take a child everywhere, if you want to. A woman who is breast-feeding a child has to hide, for example. Men can only stand breasts in porno movies or in PLAYBOY. When I was a kid in England, women would always breast-feed their babies on the tram car. A woman would be just sitting there and she would just whip it out and feed the baby and nobody would think a damn about it, except for me, who obviously noticed at ten, but it was no big deal. The fact is she was just feeding a baby. And that way women could have a baby and still do what she wanted. Now she has to hide. I don't know why breasts became such a big deal.

ONO: Breasts got *very* big. . . .

LENNON: It started with Howard Hughes. Maybe he was bottle-fed. [*Reflectively*] You know, the saying "You've come a long way baby" applies more to me than to her. As Harry Nilsson says, "Everything is the opposite of what it is, isn't it?" It's men who've come a long way from even contemplating the idea of equality. I am the one who has come a long way. I was the real pig. And it is a relief not to be a pig. The pressures of being a pig were enormous. They were killing me.

All those years of trying to be tough and the heavy rocker and heavy womanizer and heavy drinker were killing me. And it is a relief not to have to do it.

I don't have any hankerings to be looked upon as a sex object: a male, macho rock 'n' roll singer. I got over that a long time ago. I'm not even interested in projecting that. So I like it to be known that, yes, I look after the baby and I made bread and I was a househusband and I am proud of it. It was an enlightening experience for me because it was a complete reversal of my upbringing. It's the wave of the future and I'm glad to be in on the forefront of that, too.

ONO: Well, we've both come a long way.

LENNON: We both have grown, but I think I had to make a longer step. And it's still there sometimes—when there's no females in the room, there's a certain thing that happens. It's probably all right, but it still has connotations of pigsville. You know, the same macho remarks are made.

PLAYBOY: Are you in that situation often?

LENNON: No, not often.

PLAYBOY: Perhaps in the studio when Yoko is away?

LENNON: Yeah, well, that's what I was referring to.

ONO: But you come from that generation.

LENNON: Yes, I do come from that generation.

PLAYBOY: And Sean's generation?

LENNON: Well, Sean's generation is starting from scratch. We can hope. There have been changes, but even the seventeen-year-olds now are pretty much in the old bag. You see *Saturday Night Fever* and the imagery people are worshiping now. Still the basic male thing. But it's coming on. We're doing better, and that's a start.

10

Friday morning the city was gray, the sky threatening rain. Roughly a week had passed since I first entered the Dakota. As had become customary, I met John and Yoko around ten. The weather itself was inspiring that morning: John burst into the office doing a mock Gene Kelly tap dance as he crooned "Singin' in the Rain."

The limousine arrived moments later to shuttle us to the Hit Factory. The drizzle didn't faze the mob of fans who waited in a cluster outside. John signed a few autographs, posed reluctantly for a few pictures. Once beyond the doorway and into the elevator, I asked John why he was so gracious about the ever-present string of autograph and picture hounds. "It's easier to do it than to not do it," he said. He was visibly agitated by the commotion, but calmed down once upstairs sipping a Perrier and exchanging greetings with the crew.

Several hours of work later, John asked if I wanted to talk a bit while Yoko sang some background vocals. We retreated to Yoko's isolated room adjacent to the studio. After nearly two hours discussing subjects from fans to advances in recording electronics I asked John if he was ready for the inevitable Beatle-reunion question. He smiled. "Why not?"

PLAYBOY: Why is it so unthinkable that the Fab Four get back together to make some music?
LENNON: Talking about the Beatles getting back together is an illusion. That was ten years ago. The Beatles only exist on film and on record and in people's minds. You cannot get back together what no longer exists. We are not those four people anymore. Anyway,

why should I go back ten years to provide . . . to provide an illusion which I know doesn't exist.

PLAYBOY: Forget the illusion. What about just to make some music?

LENNON: Why should the Beatles give more? Didn't they give everything on God's earth for ten years? Didn't they give *themselves?* Didn't they give all?

On one hand, you're like the typical love-hate fan that says, "Thank you for everything you did for us in the Sixties. Will you give me another go, another chance? Just one more miracle? I didn't get enough the first time."

PLAYBOY: I'm playing devil's advocate. Let's clear it up once and for all. We're not talking about miracles—just good music.

LENNON: Why with the Beatles? When Rodgers worked with Hart and then he worked with Hammerstein, do you think he should have stayed only with Hart or with Hammerstein, or whoever the hell was first? Should Dean Martin have stayed with Jerry Lewis because I liked them? What's this game of doing things because other people want it? The whole Beatle idea was to do what you want, right? To take your own responsibility, do what you want and try not to harm other people, right? Do what thou wilst, as long as it doesn't hurt somebody.

PLAYBOY: All right, but back to the music itself. You don't agree that the Beatles created the best rock 'n' roll that's been produced?

LENNON: I don't. I mean, then you get into the definition of what is rock 'n' roll, what is best, all that. But the Beatles, you see—I'm too involved in them artistically. I can't listen to them objectively. I listen to them as that track, or the day we did the song. So far as I am concerned, I am dissatisfied with every record they ever fucking made. There ain't one of them I wouldn't re-make, including all the Beatles' and all my individual ones. So I cannot possibly give you an assessment of what the Beatles are.

When I was a Beatle, I thought we were the best fucking group in the goddamn world, and believing that is what made us what we were, whether you call it the best pop group or the best rock 'n' roll group or whatever. As far as we were concerned, we were the best, but we thought we were the best before anybody else had even heard of us, back in Hamburg and Liverpool. So in that respect I think the Beatles are the best thing that ever happened in pop music, but you play me those tracks and I want to remake every damn one of them. I heard "Lucy in the Sky with Diamonds" last night. It's abysmal, you know? The track is just terrible. I mean, it is a great track, a great song, but it isn't a great track because it wasn't made right. You know what I mean? I feel I could remake every fucking one of them better. But that's the artistic trip, isn't it? That is why you keep going, always trying to make that next one the best.

PLAYBOY: Some people feel that none of the songs Paul has done alone come close to the songs he came up with as a Beatle.

LENNON: So that's Paul.

PLAYBOY: How about you?

LENNON: I came up with "Imagine," "Love," and those *Plastic Ono Band* songs—they stand up to any songs that were written when I was a Beatle. Now, it may take you twenty or thirty years to appreciate that; but the fact is, these songs are as good as any fucking stuff that was ever done.

PLAYBOY: If not as commercial.

LENNON: Well, commercial. What's commercial?

PLAYBOY: Widely accepted as the best—well, as *good*.

LENNON: John Denver is commercial, so what does that mean?

PLAYBOY: But Denver has never created a song with the impact of a "Lucy in the Sky" or an "I Am the Walrus." It seems you're trying to say to the world, "We were just a good band making some good music," while a lot of people are saying, "It wasn't just some good music, it was the *best*."

LENNON: Well, if it was the best, so what?

PLAYBOY: So—

LENNON: *It can never be again!* Everyone always talks about a good thing coming to an end, as if life was over. But I'll be forty when this comes out. Paul is thirty-eight. Elton John, Bob Dylan—we're all relatively young people. The game isn't over yet. Everyone talks in terms of the last record, or the last Beatle concert—but, God willing, there are another forty years of productivity to go. Time will tell where the real magic lies.

PART TWO

PART TWO

11

Two young boys, roughly fifteen and eighteen, worked for John and Yoko running errands, answering phones, that kind of thing. Yoko had caught them one day at the front door of the upstairs apartment. They had broken into the Dakota, sneaked up the stairs and elevator, and were stumbling about the hall. Yoko heard the disturbance and surprised the boys when she angrily opened the door. "We want to meet John Lennon," one said. Yoko hung up the telephone halfway through dialing the police. Instead, she gave the boys jobs. They were good, devoted workers.

I arrived one morning and one of the boys asked me to wait for John, who was on his way downstairs to meet me. He arrived in sneakers and asked me about my weekend. We went for a walk.

Fans were waiting outside the Dakota, so John stopped me, grabbing my arm. "Follow me," he said. We tiptoed through a hall, down a creaking flight of stairs, ducking under beams. A door opened up to the Dakota's basement. Pipes dripped rusty water.

Walking through the old building's bowels, John began telling me about a sailing trip he had taken recently, an adventure about which he spoke proudly. He continued as we reached the door. John peeked outside—the path was clear. We walked up Seventy-second and down Columbus.

"It's amazing how the press will get you for what you had for lunch; but when you do something really eventful, you can get away with it," he said. "It was my first time at sea: three thousand miles, seven days.

"I'd always talked about sailing but my excuse was

91

that I never had lessons. Yoko's attitude was: 'Put up or shut up.' So she sent me on this trip and I went.

"We had talked about making music again, but she knew I would fight creating again, even though I said that I wanted to. I had said, 'Fine, but I just don't happen to have any songs.' She sent me specifically to open up my creativity, though she didn't tell me that. She knew I'd have fought it. There was four of us on this forty-one-foot boat. And it was the most fantastic experience I had ever had. I loved it!

"A storm started one afternoon and lasted three days. The captain was sick and so were his two cousins, the other guys on the boat. There was no reference point. Wherever you would look, we were the center of a circle. There was no land to be seen. They were sick and throwing up and the captain says to me, 'There's a storm coming up. Do you want to take over the wheel?' I said, 'Do you think I can?' I was supposed to be the cabinboy learning the trade, but he said, 'Well, you have to. There's no one else who can do it.' I said, 'Well, you had better keep an eye on me.' He said he would.

"Five minutes later he goes down below to sleep and says, 'See you later.' No one else could move. They were sick as dogs. So I was there, driving the boat, for six hours, keeping it on course. I was buried under water. I was smashed in the face by waves for six solid hours. It won't go away. You can't change your mind. It's like being on stage—once you're on, there's no gettin' off.

"A couple of the waves had me on my knees. I was just hanging on with my hands on the wheel—it's very powerful weather—and I was having the time of my life! I was screaming sea chanteys and shoutin' at the gods! I felt like the Viking, you know, Jason and the Golden Fleece.

"The captain found our way with a sexton. He was a great guy, Hank—how are ya, Hank, in case I didn't answer your letter! *He looked like the man on the Zig*

Zag rolling papers, with a beard and a scarf on his head, doin' the sexton. When you go on a yacht and you're in the middle of the ocean, you relive all the ocean journeys there ever were—the Vikings', Columbus's. It's incredible!

"I arrived in Bermuda. Once I got there, I was so centered after the experience at sea that I was tuned in, or whatever, to the cosmos. And all these songs came!

"The time there was just amazing. Fred [Seaman] and Sean and I were there on the beach taping songs with this big machine and me just playing guitar and singing. We were just in the sun and these songs were coming out!"

PLAYBOY: Are you ever tempted to pull up from New York and go to a place like Bermuda to live?
LENNON: No. I couldn't live anywhere that wasn't alive and kicking continually, but I have to get away more than Yoko does. She can stay in New York three hundred and sixty-five days a year. Sean and I have to get away sometimes, and if we're lucky we can drag her with us.
PLAYBOY: Do you plan to do more sailing?
LENNON: Absolutely. I would like to do the whole Atlantic, from America to England.

Over the next few days, subjects discussed were widely varied. In the studio, while Yoko was working on "Kiss Kiss Kiss," he asked me if I was satisfied with all the Beatles talk gone by. I said no; there was more to ask. "Well, let's get at it," he said, leading me to an office.

PLAYBOY: What about the suggestion that the four of you put aside your personal feelings and regroup to give a mammoth concert for charity, some sort of giant benefit? Sid Bernstein said you could raise an estimated two hundred million in one day.
LENNON: Well, first, that was a commercial for Sid Bernstein written with Jewish schmaltz and show biz

and tears, dropping on one knee, like Al Jolson. So I don't buy that. And second, I don't want to have anything to do with benefits. I have been benefited to death.

PLAYBOY: Why?

LENNON: Because they're always rip-offs. I haven't performed for personal gain since 1966, when the Beatles last performed. Every concert since then Yoko and I did for specific charities, except for a Toronto thing which was a sort of rock 'n' roll revival. Every one of the benefits was a mess or a rip-off. So now we give money to who we want. You've heard of tithing?

PLAYBOY: That's when you give away a fixed percentage of your income.

LENNON: Right. I am just going to do it privately. I am not going to get locked into that business of saving the world on stage. The show is always a mess and the artist always comes off badly.

PLAYBOY: What about the Bangladesh concert with George and Dylan and others?

LENNON: Bangladesh was caca.

PLAYBOY: Because of all the questions that were raised about where the money went?

LENNON: Yeah, right. I can't even talk about it because it's still a problem. You'll have to check with Mother [Yoko] because she knows the ins and outs of it, I don't. I will tell you that whenever people think they can get a Beatle, they can get other people—"and friends" is the big game. That means Dylan, God, Jesus, Mick, and Elton will happen to show up, too. They get a Beatle and they want to pad the show with forty other acts. They don't understand that there's always this terrible atmosphere, equipment problems, double time for the unions—the guy who is putting on the lights, carrying the bags, for promoting it—everybody else is getting paid except for the musicians. It's an absolute rip-off, but it makes the artist look good. "Isn't he a good boy!"

It's all a goddamn rip-off. So forget about it. All of

you who are reading this, don't bother sending me all that garbage about "Just come and save the Indians, come and save the blacks, come and save the war veterans." Anybody I want to save will be helped through our tithing, which is ten percent or whatever of what we earn.

And rub that "goddamn" out. I don't like that expression.

PLAYBOY: Scratch "goddamn."

LENNON [*laughing*]: Scratch "goddamn." It's a terrible expression.

PLAYBOY: Is there something you'd like to substitute?

LENNON: "Fucking." That one is better, more suited to the magazine we're in as well.

PLAYBOY: Anyway, if someone—never mind Bernstein, but someone—organized the concert so you could raise two hundred million in one day, that could do some good. Two hundred million dollars to a poverty-stricken country in South America—

LENNON: So where do people get off saying that the Beatles should give two hundred million dollars to South America? You know, America has poured billions into places like that. It doesn't mean a thing. After they've eaten that meal, then what? It only lasts for a day. After the two hundred million is gone, then what? It goes round and round in circles. You can pour money in forever. After Peru, then Harlem, then Britain. There is no one concert. We would have to dedicate the rest of our lives to one world concert tour, and I'm not ready for it. Not in this lifetime, anyway. Once you do one, everybody on earth is going to say, "Well, what's more important, people dying in Bangladesh or people dying in Harlem or people dying in Liverpool?"

PLAYBOY: Aside from the millions you've been offered for a reunion concert, how did you feel about producer Lorne Michaels's generous offer of thirty-two hundred dollars for appearing together on "Saturday Night Live" a few years ago?

LENNON: Oh, yeah, Paul and I were together watching that show. He was visiting us at our place in the Dakota. We were watching it and almost went down to the studio, just as a gag. We nearly got into a cab, but we were actually too tired.

PLAYBOY: How did you and Paul happen to be watching TV together?

LENNON: That was a period when Paul just kept turning up at our door with a guitar. I would let him in, but finally I said to him, "Please call before you come over. It's not 1956, and turning up at the door isn't the same anymore. You know, just give me a ring." He was upset by that, but I didn't mean it badly. I just meant that I was taking care of a baby all day, and some guy turns up at the door. . . . But anyway, back on that night he and Linda walked in and he and I were just sitting there watching the show, and we went, Ha-ha, wouldn't it be funny if we went down, but we didn't.

PLAYBOY: Is that the last time you've seen Paul?

LENNON: Yes, but I didn't mean it like that.

PLAYBOY: We're asking because there's always a lot of speculation about whether John, Paul, George, and Ringo are dreaded enemies or the best of friends.

LENNON: We're neither. I haven't seen *any* of the Beatles for I don't know how long. It doesn't even cross my mind as to whether I've seen them or not. It's just irrelevant. It wouldn't matter to me if I saw them often or if I never saw them again. Because the whole Beatles message was, as Baba Rama Ding-dong says, Be here now.

I don't follow what they do now. Somebody asked me what I thought of Paul's last album and I made some remark like I thought he was depressed and sad. But then I realized I hadn't listened to the whole damn thing. I heard one track—the hit, "Coming Up," which I thought was a good piece of work. Then I heard something else that sounded like he was depressed. But I don't follow their work. I don't follow Wings, you know. I don't give a shit what Wings are doing, or what

George's new album is doing or what Ringo is doing. I'm not interested, no more than I am in what Elton John or Bob Dylan is doing. It's not callousness. It's just that I'm too busy living my own life to be following what other people are doing, whether they're Beatles or guys I went to college with or people I had intense relationships with before I met the Beatles.

PLAYBOY: Besides "Coming Up," do you have an opinion on Paul's work since he left the Beatles?

LENNON: I kind of admire the way Paul started back from scratch, forming a new band and playing in small dance halls, because that's what he wanted to do with the Beatles—he wanted us to go back to the dance halls and experience that again. But I didn't . . . that was one of the problems, in a way, that he wanted to relive it all or something—I don't know what it was. . . . But I kind of admire the way he got off his pedestal—now he's back on it again, but, I mean, he did what he wanted to do. That's fine, but it's just not what I wanted to do.

PLAYBOY: You say you haven't really listened to Paul's work and haven't really talked to him since that night in your apartment—

LENNON: *Really* talked to him, no, that's the operative word. I haven't *really* talked to him in ten years. Because I haven't spent time with him. I've been doing other things and so has he. You know, he's got twenty-five kids and about twenty million records out—how can he spend time talking? He's always working.

PLAYBOY: Do you ever feel it would be interesting—forget magic, forget cosmic and all that—just *interesting* to get together with Paul with all your new experiences and cross your talents and see what happens?

LENNON: Well, would it be interesting to take Elvis back to his Sun Records period? I don't know. But I am content to listen to the Sun Records. I don't want to dig him up out of the grave. There's the talk about the magic between Lennon and McCartney, but there was magic between Rodgers and Hart, and Rodgers and Hammerstein. Lennon and McCartney and the Beatles don't exist and can never exist again. John Lennon, Paul McCartney, George Harrison, and Richard Starkey could put on a concert, but it can never be the Beatles singing "Strawberry Fields" and "I Am the Walrus" again. We cannot be that again, nor can the people who are listening.

PLAYBOY: Sure, but perhaps simply for old times' sake, like a high-school reunion?

LENNON: I never went to high-school reunions. My thing is, Out of sight, out of mind. That's my attitude toward life. So I don't have any romanticism about any part of my past. I think of it only inasmuch as it gave me pleasure or helped me grow psychologically. That is the only thing that interests me about yesterday. I *don't* believe in yesterday [*chuckles*], by the way. You know *I don't believe in yesterday*. I am only interested in what I am doing now.

I never went to see Elvis, although I had the opportunity to see him and I *worshiped* him the way people worshiped the Beatles. Because when I was sixteen, Elvis was what was happening. A guy with long hair wiggling his ass and singing "Hound Dog" and "That's All Right" and all those great early Sun Records, which I think are his *great* period. But I didn't go see him, because there's no way he could have been that again. Never mind that he was fat and drugged and all that. Even if he *wasn't* fat and drugged, he couldn't have been that guy who sang "That's All Right" again. A friend of mine, a *big* Elvis fan, *bigger* than I was, went to see him. I wouldn't go, because I knew it wasn't him. He was not the one who made the other records. Not that he started making stupid movies and all the intellectual reasons why I wouldn't go see him, but because it couldn't be him. When he saw him in Vegas, I asked my friend how he was. He said, "Well, if you sort of half shut your eyes and pretended, it was heaven."

I'm not interested in half shutting my eyes and pretending it was heaven to watch Elvis or creating that kind of situation for other people. I am only interested in now and what I am doing now. I will talk about the Beatles forever and ever. I will discuss them intellectually and what they mean and what they don't mean. That doesn't bother me. What does is the idea that people think we can re-create it for them—for the kids who keep writing me saying, "I'm only fourteen now and I missed it." I think that's pathetic. I mean *forget* about that. Listen to the Beatles records, but dig Queen or Clash or whatever is going on now.

And for the ones who want to relive it, "Resurrect the Beatles" and all, for those who didn't understand the Beatles and the Sixties in the first place, what the fuck are we going to do for them now? [*Passionately, rhythmically*] Do we have to divide the fish and the loaves for the multitudes again? Do we have to get crucified *again?* Do we have to do the walking on water *again* because a whole pile of dummies didn't *see* it the first time or didn't believe it when they saw it? That's what they're asking: "Get off the cross. I didn't understand it the first time. Can you do it again?" *No way!* You can't do things twice. What's that thing? You can never go home. It doesn't exist. It's not that we're *withholding* it from you; we don't possess it to withhold it. It was never ours in the first place. It existed of its own.

This moaning about Beatles is the same as our parents who never stopped talking about the goddamn Second World War. Yes, it was very important, but not to us. We used to get "We never had that in the war" and "We didn't have matches during the war. We didn't have milk. . . ." Too bad, but I've got it. That's all I ever heard from home! I don't know what it was like in America, but all we ever heard as kids in England was how lucky we were because of the fucking war.

Well, that is *over,* man. The war is over and the Sixties is over and the Beatles is over and it's all the same. I'm not against the war or the Beatles or Paul,

George, and Ringo. I've no ax to grind either way, but I don't want to go to the reunion with Japanese fighter planes. I don't want to be one of those people meeting around the Messerschmitts and the Spitfires reliving World War II. *I'm not interested* in it, okay? It's just irrelevant, *absolutely irrelevant*.

12

PLAYBOY: What about those who maintain that without the Beatles there'd be no rock 'n' roll as we know it?

LENNON: Without rock 'n' roll there would be no Beatles. It's all speculation. Without Elvis there would be no Beatles. Without Johnny Ray there would be no Elvis. Without whoever came before Johnny Ray there would be no Johnny Ray. It's endless. It's timeless. In the Sixties it was the Beatles, so that music is going to be important to them until they die. But in the Forties it was, whatever, Glenn Miller, and when our parents hear Glenn Miller they go through the same thing. Maybe they didn't put all the extra stuff on it, though, as our generation did. You know, all the cosmic stuff.

PLAYBOY: What do you say to those who insist all rock since the Beatles has been the Beatles redone?

LENNON: *All* music is rehash. There are only a few notes. Just variations on a theme. Try to tell the kids in the Seventies who were screaming to the Bee Gees that their music is just the Beatles redone. There is nothing wrong with the Bee Gees. They do a damn good job. There was nothing else going on then.

PLAYBOY: Wasn't a lot of the Beatles at least more intelligent?

LENNON: The Beatles were more intellectual, so they

appealed on that level, too. But the basic appeal of the Beatles was not their intelligence. It was their music. It was only after some guy in the *London Times* said there were aeolian cadences in "It Won't Be Long" that the middle classes started listening to it—because somebody put a tag on it.

PLAYBOY: *Did* you put aeolian cadences in "It Won't Be Long"?

LENNON: To this day I don't have *any* idea what they are. They sound like exotic birds.

PLAYBOY: So how did you react to all the misinterpretations of your songs?

LENNON: For instance?

PLAYBOY: The most obvious is the "Paul is dead" fiasco. What about the line in "I Am the Walrus": "I buried Paul"?

LENNON: I said, "Cranberry sauce." [*As on the record*] Cranberry sauce. That's all I said.

PLAYBOY: There was no intent in any of the "Paul is dead" thing?

LENNON: How can there be intent in cranberry sauce?

PLAYBOY: But what about "Here's another clue for you all, the walrus is Paul" from "Glass Onion"?

LENNON: Well, that was a joke. The line was put in partly because I was feeling guilty because I was with Yoko and I was leaving Paul. I was trying—I don't know. It's a very perverse way of saying to Paul, you know, "Here, have this crumb, this illusion, this—this stroke, because I'm leaving."

PLAYBOY: Were you amused by the "Paul is dead" thing when everyone was playing your records backward and crying?

LENNON: They all had a good time. It was meaningless.

PLAYBOY: What about the chant at the end of "Walrus": "Smoke pot, smoke pot, everybody smoke pot"?

LENNON: No, no, no. I had this whole choir saying "Everybody's got one, everybody's got one." But when you get thirty people, male and female, on top of thirty cellos and on top of the Beatles' rock 'n' roll rhythm section, you can't hear what they're saying.

PLAYBOY: What *does* "everybody got"?

LENNON: Anything. You name it. One penis, one vagina, one asshole—you name it.

PLAYBOY: Nothing about smoking pot?

LENNON: I wouldn't be so gross. Listen, writing about music is like talking about fucking. Who wants to talk about it? But you know, maybe some people do want to talk about it. Fucking is fucking, and not fucking is not fucking.

PLAYBOY: What about when it goes as far as Charles Manson claiming that your lyrics were messages to him?

LENNON: It has nothing to do with me. It's like that guy, Son of Sam, who was having these talks with a dog. Manson was just an extreme version of the people who came up with the "Paul is dead" thing or who figured out that the initials to "Lucy in the Sky with Diamonds" were LSD.

PLAYBOY: It's hard to misinterpret the songs you're doing now.

LENNON: I'm not interested in creating illusion. *Plastic Ono* was simple and straight. That is what I am trying to do. I am always trying to do that. I just want to say direct whatever I am trying to say. I'm not interested in poetry with a capital "P." To me the best poetry is haiku. All the best paintings are Zen. The less said, the better. I would like to be able to say it without lyrics, but I can't. I'm just—just verbal. Somehow it is clarity that I am looking for, clarity of expression. Painting wallpaper or making Muzak is not what I want to do, although I have nothing against it. I'm just trying to put a clear moment on canvas.

If people don't like it, well . . . It's the same as wanting the Beatles back. You want music from me, you'll get it. But don't tell me which music to make or suggest how I do it. Otherwise, you go do it yourself. There's room for everybody. Somebody else can go do that.

PLAYBOY: And people have.

LENNON: And people have, right. I mean E.L.O. is son of "I Am the Walrus." If somebody wants "I Am the Walrus" music, they just have to buy E.L.O. records. Different schools of "Son of Beatles" exist continually.

PLAYBOY: Do you find that the clamor for a Beatles reunion has died down?

LENNON: Well, I heard some Beatles stuff on the radio the other day and I heard "Green Onion"—no, "Glass Onion"—I don't even know my own songs! I listened to it because it was a rare track. It's a song they usually don't play. When a radio station has a Beatles weekend, they usually play the same ten songs—"A Hard Day's Night," "Help!" "Yesterday," "Something," "Let It Be"—you know, there's all that wealth of material, but we hear only ten songs. So the deejay says, "I want to thank John, Paul, George, and Ringo for *not* getting back together and spoiling a good thing." I thought it was a good sign. Maybe people are catching on.

PLAYBOY: Pop historians spend a lot of time analyzing "the Beatles phenomenon" and the dynamics of the band—your personalities, Brian Epstein's secret love of Paul . . .

LENNON: It's irrelevant. He wasn't in love with Paul. He was in love with me. It's irrelevant, you know.

PLAYBOY: It doesn't interest you?

LENNON: It's irrelevant. I will read anything that comes out—I like archeology, anthropology, anything ancient like that. I love it. I would dig going on a dig. [*Laughs*] But everybody has their own place. Mine is to do, and other people's is to record. I can't do both. I mean, who cares whether Glenn Miller was killed by the CIA or the Nazis or what the hell? The point is he's dead. Does it matter how many drugs were in Elvis's body? I mean, it's interesting and it will make a nice *Hollywood Babylon* someday about Brian Epstein's sex life, but it's irrelevant, absolutely irrelevant.

PLAYBOY: How about the psychoanalyses of why you do what you do?

LENNON: It's only games for people to play. Some people like Ping-Pong, other people like digging over graves. They are all escapes from now. People will do anything rather than be here now. It's irrelevant. If some people want to do it, let them do it. They put all their fantasies on other people, whether it's the Beatles or Elvis or Glenn Miller.

The door opened and Yoko poked her head in, asking how everything was going. She said she was finished and wondered if we were ready to leave. After munching on the sushi and sashimi—"dead fish," as John called it—that was delivered daily from a Columbus Avenue Japanese restaurant, we rode in the waiting car back to the Dakota. It had grown dark outside and Yoko rested her head wearily on John's shoulder.

13

Inside, John peered up and down the halls. He winked at me. "He's around here somewhere." Finally, from behind us, Sean came charging down the hall, plowing headfirst into his father's outstretched arms. As John said, Sean was truly beautiful, radiant dark eyes— sometimes they were John's, sometimes Yoko's—peering from a sticky face smeared with chocolate. John teased Sean about the mess as he carried him to the kitchen. Yoko had disappeared to another part of the house.

John introduced me, and Sean politely said hello. Soon Sean was on John's lap talking about "birdies" and "paper things" he wanted to show us. He ran into the other room and returned, red-cheeked and excited, with small paper birds and a fingerpainting. He dropped the picture in John's lap and pulled himself up on mine. "See?" he asked, holding up his creation. He said he wanted to make more so the bird wouldn't be alone and they could fly together in his room. "But I'll close the door so they won't fly away and get lost," he said giggling.

John praised the picture, and when Yoko came in Sean popped off my lap to run up for a hug. Soon it was bedtime. Sean pleaded a bit for an extra few minutes, then reluctantly grabbed John's hand to be led away.

When John returned, we chatted about the day. John and Yoko talked over some points about the record— should it be called "An Ear Play" or was that too much, or perhaps "A Heart Play," since the word "Heart" contained the word "Ear"?—until it was time to continue. I diffidently asked if we could return to more Beatle talk. Yoko laughed, "Of course." John groaned.

PLAYBOY: For the sake of argument, let's maintain that no other group of artists moved as many people in such a profound way as the Beatles.

LENNON: *But what moved the Beatles?*

PLAYBOY: You tell me.

LENNON: All right. Whatever wind was blowing at the time moved the Beatles too. I'm not saying we weren't flags on the top of the ship. But the whole boat was moving. Maybe the Beatles were in the crow's nest shouting "Land Ho!" or something like that, but we were all in the same damn boat. You can't go through life looking at the crow's nest. Somebody has to pull the sails up and down.

PLAYBOY: Say the Beatles *were* merely the crow's nest. Then it makes sense that people look up toward it again.

ONO: But the Beatles themselves were a social phenomenon not that aware of what they were doing. In a way . . .

LENNON [*under his breath*]: This Beatles talk bores me to death. Turn to page 196.

ONO: I am sure there are people whose lives are affected because they heard Indian music or Mozart or Bach. More than anything it was the time and the place when the Beatles came up. Something did happen there. It was a kind of chemical. It was as if several people gathered around a table and a ghost appeared. It was that kind of communication. So they were like mediums in a way. It was more than four people. They had something going, a strong attachment to each other, a feeling of being together. Now it's different. It's not something you can force. It was the people, the time, their youth and enthusiasm. As I said, they were like mediums. They weren't conscious of all they were saying but it was coming through them.

PLAYBOY: Why?

LENNON: We tuned in to the message. That's all. I don't mean to belittle the Beatles when I say they weren't this, they weren't that. I'm just trying not to overblow their importance as separate from society. And I don't think they were more important than Glenn Miller or Woody Herman or Bessie Smith. It was our generation, that's all. It was Sixties music.

ONO: And people want more? Just remember, when you go through the Bible, Christ was around for five years. He conveniently got on the cross, saying, I'm going to do it again, but the Beatles did it for ten years—that's enough, right?

LENNON: Don't you think the Beatles did enough of everything? It took our whole life, a whole section of our youth; during a time when everybody else was just goofing off and smoking dope, *we* were working twenty-four hours a day. I was doing it and doing it and doing it and there was no switching off. The elevator man wanted a little piece of you on your way back to the hotel room, the maid wanted a little piece of you back at the hotel—I don't mean sexually, I mean a piece of your time and your energy. And so it dawns on me: Am I going back into that? And while we're at it, we have to get this Beatle thing straight about the Beatles saving the world. If you don't see it, nobody is going to. Giving money we raised by getting back together is giving someone aspirin for a headache. The cause of the headache is not going to be solved.

PLAYBOY: Maybe you don't give aspirin. Maybe you raise the money and do something different—establish social programs, whatever.

LENNON: But why me? Why not you? Why don't you start right now and get yourself as famous as the Beatles? It's quite easy if you want to work twenty-four hours a day and keep smiling and dancing for ten to fifteen years. Then *you* can do it. Why is everybody telling me to do it? I already did it! We've done God knows how many benefits. We were there to provide whatever the Beatles provided. We are not there to save the fucking world.

ONO: Also, the money that would be generated would not be what you would think. The tax problems are enough, but a lot of people—the money would not go to the proper place that you would want it to do. And there is the idea that these four male figures, or an extension of these four male figures, have done some good things and that on a symbolic level a concert might work, but in a practical sense, on a money level, it usually doesn't work. And they have experience at that, believe me.

PLAYBOY: On the subject of your own wealth, the *New York Post* recently said you admitted to being worth a hundred and fifty million.

LENNON: We never admitted anything.

PLAYBOY: The *Post* said you had.

LENNON: What the *Post* says— Okay, so we are rich, so what?

PLAYBOY: Well, the question is, how does that jibe with your political philosophies?

LENNON: In England there are only two things to be, basically: You are either for the labor movement or for the capitalist movement. You either become a right-wing Archie Bunker if you were in the class I am in, or you become an instinctive socialist, which I was. That meant I think people should get their false teeth and their health looked after, all the rest of it. But apart from that, I worked for money and I wanted to be rich. So what the hell. If that's a paradox, then I'm not a socialist. What the hell. But I am not *anything*. I was instinctively for the workers because that was the people I was living with, although lots of workers are right-wing. What I used to be was guilty about money. That's why I lost it, either by giving it away or allowing myself to be screwed by so-called managers, or whatever you call them. But subconsciously it was because I was guilty about having money.

PLAYBOY: Because?

LENNON: Because I thought money was equated with sin. I don't know. I think I got over it, because I either have to put up or shut up, you know. If I'm going to be a monk with nothing, do it. Otherwise, if I am going to try and make money, make it. Money itself isn't the root of all evil. Money is just a concept; also it's just energy. So now you could say I've come to terms with money and making money.

I always ignored it. So now Yoko looks after the business, parlaying money into things like cows and real estate. Between us we had to face the reality that the money was there, and I always avoided that. I am too artistic to deal with money in any way, basically. I am a socialist who just happens to be getting this money. Ignoring it always caused me problems. I'm having a hard time explaining it. I'm a bit slow now because I'm tired. I have to kind of collect my thoughts about it.

PLAYBOY: We can come back to it.

LENNON: No, it's all right. If we keep pushing, we will make sense.

It's not that I'm above politics, it's that politics isn't what I do. Politics is separate from society, while I'm not. Politics is inclusive, like art and eating and having babies; it's not just something you do every four years.

As Gore Vidal often quotes, "Don't vote for them, it only encourages them." I have never voted for anybody, anytime, ever. Even at my most so-called political. I have never registered and I never will. It's going to make a lot of people upset, but that's too bad. I'm with the majority. The majority don't vote. Well, they know better.

ONO: There is no denying that we are still living in a capitalist world, and in order for us to survive in this world we must take care of ourselves. We have friends that are sort of socialists from the 1920s, born with money, always saying they don't care about money. It's very easy to do. But I think that in order to survive and in order to change the world, first of all you have to take care of yourself. You have to survive yourself. To change the society you have to deal with the particular society. . . .

Now a lot of people in the Sixties went underground and thought of bombing the White House, whatever. That's the violent method, which I think has too much repercussion, and it doesn't result in anything. So that is not the way, definitely not for me.

If you don't use violence and you don't want money, you don't have power to do anything. So if you do want to change the system, become a part of the system with a position to change it. So you need money. Even if you want to be a mayor or something.

It is sad that in this society if you don't think about money, you become a parasite. In some societies, even if you don't think about money and if you are an artist or you have skills, that's all you need—and that's not referring to Soviet Russia, because their system is defective also. I'm not saying that there is a society in the world right now that exists in that sense at all. It's the idealism in everybody to think that there should be such a thing in society to protect the people so that they don't have to really depend on the money system. But this society is dependent on the money system. So we have to play that game.

LENNON: "No messages from any phony politician are coming through me." I said that earlier and it's still true. That still stands. I dabbled in so-called politics in the late Sixties and Seventies more out of guilt than anything. Guilt for being rich, and guilt thinking that perhaps love and peace isn't enough and you have to go and get shot or something, or get punched in the face, to prove I'm one of the people. I was doing it against my instincts.

ONO [*recites*]: "Now, I am the only socialist living here. [*She laughs.*] I don't have a penny. It's all John's, so that's fine." I used to really play that game. But the money, of course, is a part of me, too; I am using the money as well and have to face that. So, yes, you have to play the money game.

PLAYBOY: To what extent do you play the game without getting caught up in it—money for the sake of money, in other words?

ONO: There is a limit. It would probably be parallel to our level of security. Do you know what I mean? I mean the emotional-security level.

PLAYBOY: Has it reached that level yet?

ONO [*laughs*]: No, not yet. I don't know. It might have, but we feel more comfortable with that.

PLAYBOY: You mean with a hundred and fifty million? Is that an accurate estimate?

ONO: I don't know what we have. When it becomes so complex that you need to have ten accountants working for two years to find out what you have, I really can't say anything about it. But let's say we feel comfortable now. Comfortable and independent. And we give our ten percent of our income to the needy.

PLAYBOY: How have you chosen to invest your money?

ONO: To make money, you have to spend money. But if you are going to make money, you have to make it with love. I love Egyptian art. I make sure I get all the Egyptian things, not for their value but for their magic power. Each piece has a certain magic power. Also with houses. I just buy ones we love, not the ones that people say are good investments.

PLAYBOY: The papers have made it sound as if you are buying up the Atlantic seaboard.

ONO: When you see the houses, you would understand. They do become an investment, but they are not an investment unless you sell them. Each house is like a historic landmark and they're very beautiful. We're really in love with each house.

PLAYBOY: Do you actually use all the properties?

ONO: Most people would have the park to go and run—the park is a huge place—but John and I were never able to go to the park together, or not very much, you know. So we have to create our own parks.

PLAYBOY: We heard that you own sixty million dollars' worth of dairy cows. Could that be true?

ONO: I don't know. I'm not a calculator. I'm not going by figures, I'm going by the excellence of things.

PLAYBOY: For an artist, your business sense seems remarkable.

ONO: I was doing it just like laying out a chess game. And I love chess. I do this and everything like a chess game. Not on a Monopoly level—that's a bit more realistic. Chess is more conceptual.

PLAYBOY: John, do you really need all these houses around the country so you can have a place to get away?

LENNON: They're good business, but we do love them and use them.

PLAYBOY: Why does anyone need a hundred and fifty million dollars? Couldn't you be perfectly content with a hundred million? Or one million?

LENNON: What would you suggest I do? Give everything away and walk the streets? I wasn't content with *no* dollars, I wasn't content with a million, and I'm not content with a hundred million. Contentment doesn't lie in money.

PLAYBOY: Then why be in the game of getting more?

LENNON: Because to do what I do, I need what money does.

PLAYBOY: A hundred and fifty million?

LENNON: It's all relative, isn't it?

PLAYBOY: What about all the talk of transcending possessions?

LENNON: You can transcend possessions without walking around in a robe. Possessions can be in the mind. A monk who's off in a cave dreaming about fucking, sucking, and eating is in a far worse position than me who has so-called money in his back pocket. I'm over the conflict that says you can't be awake and have money. That's absolute rubbish. When Christ said, "It's as easy for a rich man to get to heaven as to go through the eye of a needle," I took it literally—that one has to dump possessions to get through to nirvana, or whatever you call it. But an intellectual has less chance of getting through than me. They're possessed of ideas. An intellectual with no money who's living the ascetic life—no TV and all that—well, they're possessed of ideas, ideas of what they're supposed to be. I'm no longer possessed of ideas. So those were the possessions I had to get rid of; not the physical possessions.

ONO: One cannot get rid of things by repressing. In order to get "rid," you have to first "get," you know?

LENNON: My insecurity is having too many clothes. That's a physical manifestation of my insecurity—a closet full of clothes I cannot possibly wear. But I understand it. I still have the clothes and I still dump them on the Salvation Army once a year, whatever. But I understand the neurosis. But having a lot of money is no longer a problem for me. That's why we ended up with more. Yoko didn't have that problem, because she was born rich and she was rich all her life. She couldn't understand my attitude about money. Whether we had more or less seemed irrelevant to her.

So possessions are not just physical possessions. Possessions are ideas. Most people are choked to death by concepts and ideas that they carry around with them, usually not their own but their parents' and society's. Those are the possessions you've got to get rid of to get through the eye of the needle. It has absolutely nothing to do with physical possessions.

PLAYBOY: Are you through the eye of the needle?

LENNON: I think I've been through it and back a few times. What the hell do I know? I do know it's not a matter of how much gold you have in your pocket. There are many awakened very rich people and many awakened people who don't physically own anything. One bowl, one cup. What is it? The Zen thing? One bowl, one cloak. For me to do that would be pretty crazy—to just walk away from it all. That means no possessions, including your family and ties and everything. That's *that* extreme. But to walk away would be walking away from responsibility. It's like the Beatles. I can't walk away from the Beatles. That's one possession that's still tagging along, right? No matter what I say. If I walk away from what I am, whether it's two houses or four hundred houses, I'm not gonna escape it.

PLAYBOY: How do you escape it?

LENNON: It takes time to get rid of all this garbage that I've been carrying around that was influencing the way I thought and the way I lived. It had a lot to do with Yoko, showing me that I was still possessed. I left physically when I fell in love with Yoko, but mentally it took the last ten years of struggling. I learned everything from her.

14

PLAYBOY: You make your relationship with Yoko sound like a teacher-pupil relationship.

LENNON: It *is* a teacher-pupil relationship. That's what people don't understand. She's the teacher and I'm the pupil. I'm the famous one, the one who's supposed to know everything, but she's my teacher. She's taught me everything I fucking know. She was there when I was nowhere, when I was the *nowhere man*. She's my Don Juan [a reference to Carlos Castaneda's Yaqui Indian teacher]. That's what people don't understand. I'm married to fucking Don Juan, that's the hardship of it. She's the one who told me to find a place to sit. And Don Juan doesn't have to laugh; Don Juan doesn't have to be charming; Don Juan just is. And what goes on around Don Juan is irrelevant to Don Juan.

It's like when she told me to get out—Don Ono said "Get out" because you're not getting it. Well, it was like being sent into the desert. And the reason she wouldn't let me back in was because I wasn't *ready* to come back in yet. And when I was ready to come back in, she let me back in. And that's what I'm living with.

PLAYBOY: Yoko, how do you feel about being John's teacher?

ONO: Well, he had a lot of experience before he met me, the kind of experience I never had, so I learned a lot from him, too. It's both ways. Maybe it's that I have strength, a feminine strength. Because women develop it. In a relationship I think women really have the inner wisdom and they're carrying that, while men have sort of the wisdom to cope with society, since they created it. Men never developed the inner wisdom; they didn't have time. So most men do rely on women's inner wisdom, whether they express that or not. I think John is simply expressing that. Even to say it shows he understands. It's supposed to be a sissy thing to say "I learned a lot from a woman."

PLAYBOY: What's the difference between following Yoko and the other kinds of leaders? "Don't follow leaders. . . ."?

LENNON: What's the difference between Don Juan and not Don Juan? What's the difference between illusion and reality? It's *that* different. She has absolutely never looked for *other* since I met her.

PLAYBOY: But it sounds like Yoko has become John's guru.

LENNON: No, a Don Juan doesn't have a following. A Don Juan isn't in the newspaper and doesn't have disciples and doesn't need anything and doesn't proselytize or propagate. Those who know don't say, and those who say don't know.

Her Indica Gallery show was like meeting Don Juan. At first I didn't realize who I was meeting. Then, because I got the initial game, I played the initial game and we connected.

PLAYBOY: Will you recount the story of the meeting of the wondrous mystic prince and Don Ono?

LENNON: It was in 1966 in England. I'd been told about this "event"—

[There is a shrill scream from outside]

Oh, another murder at rue Dakota. . . . *[Laughter]*

—this "event," a Japanese avant-garde artist coming from America. She was red-hot. There was going to be something about black bags, and I thought it was all gonna be sex: artsy-fartsy orgies. Great! Well, it was far out, but it was not the way I thought it was going to be.

So I walked in and there's nobody there. It turns out that it was the night before opening night. The place wasn't really opened, but John Dunbar, the owner, was all nervous, like, "The millionaire's come to buy something!" He's flittering around like crazy. Now I'm looking at this stuff. There's a couple of nails on a plastic box. Then I look over and see an apple on a stand—a fresh apple on a stand with a note saying "apple." I thought, you know, This is a joke, this is pretty funny. *[Yoko laughs remembering the day]*.

I was beginning to see the humor of it. I said, "How much is the apple?" "Two hundred pounds? Really. Oh, I see. So how much are the bent nails?"

So I was wandering around having a good time and I went downstairs and there's just a couple of scruffy people sitting around in jeans. I was feeling a bit defensive, thinking, They must be the hip ones. But no, it turns out they were just assistants putting all this stuff together for her. But I was, like, I'm the famous, rich pop star and these must be the ones that know what those nails and apples are all about. I took it humorously, which turned out to be fine, but I was sort of reacting like a lot of people react to her humor, which is—they get angry at her and say she's got no sense of humor. Actually, she's hysterically funny.

So anyway, this goes on for a bit, and then Dunbar brings her over because, you know, the *millionaire* is here, right.

ONO: [Dunbar] didn't say anything to me. He just dragged me out.

LENNON: And I'm waiting for the bag. Where's the people in the *bag,* you know? All the time I was thinking about whether I'd have the nerve to get in the bag with whoever. You know, you don't know who's gonna be in the bag.

So he introduced me, and of course there was supposed to be this event happening, so I asked, "Well, what's the event?" She gives me a little card. It just says "Breathe" on it. And I said, "You mean [*panting*]?" She says, "That's it. You've got it." And I'm thinking, I've got it! [*Laughs*] But I'm all geared up to *do* something. I want to do something.

ONO: Well, you did it.

LENNON: I did the breathing, but I wanted more than, you know, putting my consciousness on my breathing, which is an intellectual way of looking at it. I saw the nails and I got the humor—maybe I didn't get the depth of it, but I got a warm feeling from it. I thought, *Fuck,* I can make that. I can put an apple on a stand. I want more.

But then I saw this ladder on a painting leading up to the ceiling where there was a spyglass hanging down. It's what made me stay. I went up the ladder and I got the spyglass and there was tiny little writing there. You really have to stand on the top of the ladder, like this [*John gets up and acts it out*]. You're on this ladder—you feel like a fool—you could fall any minute—and you look through and it just says "YES."

Well, all the so-called avant-garde art at the time and everything that was supposedly interesting was all negative, this smash-the-piano-with-a-hammer, break-the-sculpture boring, negative crap. It was all anti-, anti-, anti. Anti-art, anti-establishment. And just that "YES" made me stay in a gallery full of apples and nails instead of just walking out saying, "I'm not gonna buy any of this crap."

Then I went up to this thing that said, "Hammer a nail in." I said, "Can I hammer a nail in?" and she said no, because the gallery was actually opening the next day. So the owner, Dunbar, says, "Let him hammer a nail in." It was "He's a millionaire. He might buy it," you know. She's more interested in it looking nice and pretty and white for the opening. That's why she never made any money on the stuff; she's always too busy protecting it. [*Laughing*]

So there was this little conference and she finally said, "Okay, you can hammer a nail in for five shillings." So smart-ass here says, "Well, I'll give you an imaginary five shillings and hammer an imaginary nail in." And that's when we really *met*. That's when we locked eyes and she got it and I got it and that was it. The rest, as they say in all the interviews we do, is history.

PLAYBOY: What happened to those pieces?

LENNON: I'll show them to you. They're in the house. Sean and I put an apple on the stand now and then, but Sean always eats it.

ONO [*smiling*]: We were both married, of course. But we were dating.

LENNON: Which is when things began to change. That's when I started to free myself from the Beatles. And that's when everybody started getting a bit upset. . . .

ONO: Even now, I just read that Paul said, "I understand that he wants to be with her, but why does he have to be with her all the time?''

LENNON: Yoko, do you still have to carry that cross? That was years ago.

ONO: No, no, no. He said it recently. I mean, what happened with John is that I sort of went to bed with this guy that I liked and suddenly the next morning I see these three guys standing there with resentful eyes.

PLAYBOY: Do you think that kind of attitude from people was also jealousy?

LENNON: It's a kind of jealousy. People can't stand people being in love. They absolutely can't stand it. They want to pull you down in the hole they're in.

PLAYBOY: Doesn't the good feeling rub off?

LENNON: Well, yeah, but wait till you don't want them in the room with you. It's your self-absorption with each other; it's your contentment with each other that people can't stand. Of course they're attracted to you because your energy is positive and high—of the highest form. But energy attracts energy suckers. Whether they come in the guise of friend or enemy is irrelevant. That's why the line [in "Watching the Wheels"] "No friends and no enemies." It comes in many mysterious forms. They'll suck you dry. That's what the game is. It's hard enough to make it stay.

PLAYBOY: As Tom Robbins half-facetiously asks in his most recent book, "How *do* you make love stay?''

LENNON: Trying to possess it makes it go away. Trying to possess somebody makes them go away. Every time you put your finger on it, it slips away. Every time you turn the microscope's light on, the thing changes so you can never see what it is. As soon as you ask the question, it goes away. Peripheral vision is what it is. There's no looking directly at it. Try to look at the sun. You go blind, right? Now that doesn't mean you don't have to work on it. Love is a flower and you have to water it.

ONO: Yes. I think that love will never die. Once you know somebody, you can never unknow that person.

And knowing is loving. So you can never get out of love. There might be misunderstandings and separating for other reasons, but love is always there. Staying together is just one form of love. Maybe that's a strong love and expression of love. But love is a soul thing. It always stays there. I don't think people should be insecure about falling out of love. If they're not afraid of love, then they're always going to love. Everybody's got love and that's why they want to know how to make love last and all that. Everybody's really concerned about love. It's the biggest issue. Love makes everything work. It makes everything grow.

It's hard, too. Sometimes we feel possessive, and that's fine. We shouldn't be ashamed of these feelings we have. It's fine. We're so ashamed of being jealous; so ashamed of being possessive. We're so afraid of having hate and all that. We shouldn't. It's all just different forms of energy. Energy goes through different forms. Nothing that we possess is ugly. Everything that comes out of us is beautiful. We're taught that singing a song is beautiful, but if you sing out of tune it's not beautiful. We're taught you have to sing a certain way. But I think everything that comes out of us is beautiful because we're human.

I'm amazed at what people are. How resilient they are! They're born with no assurance that they'll survive. Their assurance are parents who are so insecure that they, themselves, are like children. And *they survive*. They survive all the "Don't do this, don't do that." The "You're not supposed to do this." It's exciting to think what someone without those insecurities that we've grown up with might be able to do, but even with them *we survive*. Imagine really *knowing* it's all right. [*Smiling and shaking her head*] Life is so hard anyway. It's very courageous to keep going. To say in spite of it all we had a good life. [*Laughing*] I think life is beautiful and I enjoy it. I am enjoying it.

In the end maybe I'm an endless optimist. I think of those people thinking, "Oh, well, the world is going to end very soon so I won't have children." Well, if you're afraid of losing, you're going to lose. Look at the people. We're talking about how beautiful the world is—and it's true.

LENNON: Well, today it is. Yesterday it was terrible. So what the hell. [*He and Yoko laugh*]

ONO: It's like that. It's okay. If you know that, you won't be so frightened. If you're not so frightened, love will stay.

15

PLAYBOY: Why did you decide to marry?

LENNON: Because we're romantic. And there *was* a difference. The same way the divorce didn't seem like a divorce until they gave you the papers, I suppose. No matter what the intellectual thing is—we lived together for two or three years—when the divorce papers went through and they said, "You are free," we felt free. Intellectually we know it's all bullshit, but getting married was at least as important as getting divorced.

ONO: We really wanted to get married. It was a statement and a commitment.

LENNON: Also, rituals *are* important, no matter what we thought as kids. [*Mockingly*] "Marriage—ha-ha-ha." So nowadays it's hip not to be married. But I'm not interested in being hip. That is, I'm interested in being hip with a capital "H," not fashionable.

PLAYBOY: And after your wedding came the bed-in.

LENNON: Right. When we got married, we knew our honeymoon was going to be public anyway, so we decided to use it to make a statement. Our life is our art. That's what the bed-in was. We sat in bed and talked to reporters for seven days. It was hilarious. In effect, we were doing a commercial for peace instead of a commercial for war. The reporters were going "uh-huh, yeah, sure," but it didn't matter because our commercial went out irrespective. As I've said, everybody puts down TV commercials, but they go around singing them.

At the bed-in one guy kept going over the point about Hitler: "What do you do about fascists? How can you have peace when you've got a Hitler?" Yoko said, "I would have gone to bed with him." She said she'd only have needed ten days with him. People loved that one.

ONO: I said it facetiously, of course. But the point is you're not going to change the world by fighting. Maybe I was naïve about the ten days with Hitler. After all, it took thirteen years with John Lennon. [*She giggles*].

PLAYBOY: What about the reports about you making love in a bag?

ONO: We never made love in a bag. People probably imagined that we were making love. It was just, all of us are in a bag, you know. The point was the outline of the bag, the movement of the bag: how much we see of a person. Inside there might be a lot going on. Or maybe nothing's going on.

PLAYBOY: With the stir you cause going public and the serenity you apparently have away from the public, why do you choose to do those things—art statements, records, whatever—publicly?

ONO: Everything is public. Whatever you're doing, even if you cough or sneeze or something, is going to affect the world. Even things you think you are doing in private. We're all sharing the whole world together. There is no reason why you can't do these things publicly. On the contrary, you *have* to do it publicly.

LENNON: It's like what I was saying before about the bed-ins. We knew we would be followed by the press after we got married anyway, so we sat down and said, "What use can we make of the situation that would be interesting, a nice projection of what *can be?*" We asked, "How can we utilize the situation we are in?" So we had our honeymoon in public.

ONO: And, you know, the bed-ins were a part of the whole time of protests that changed the world. For all the negative aspects of the time, it really did change the world. People were resisting what was going on. That was the saving grace of it. And we were just a part of it.

PLAYBOY: Political statements must be made publicly, but what about far more personal statements: "Dear Yoko," "Oh Yoko," from John, and Yoko's songs about him. You've received a lot of criticism about that.

ONO: If we write love songs, it's because we were feeling love. It wasn't like, "Oh, let's put some love songs in it, too." The album reflects our life, so there is some love and there is some fear.

LENNON: You write about what you know, at least I do. There is no line between private and public. There is no line. "Everybody's got something to hide except me and my monkey." There *is* nothing to hide, really. We all like to shit in private and we have certain little things that we prefer to do privately, but, in general, what is there to hide? What's the big secret? The secret is there is no secret.

16

John's assistant rang my phone one morning. "John wants to know how fast you can meet him at the apartment!" It was a short cab ride away. He was waiting downstairs. He briefed me: "A guy's trying to serve me a subpoena and I don't want to deal with it. Will you help me out?" ["Just what I need, another law suit,"

*sighed John.] First he asked me to check the path from
the building to the waiting limousine. It was clear. I
gave him a nod and he dashed by me, falling into the
back seat of the car, and I stumbled in on top of him.
John had the driver streak toward the studio; it was
three hours before he was due to arrive.*

*As we approached the studio, John told the driver to
slow to a crawl and he instructed me to lead the way
inside after making sure the coast was clear. "If anybody comes up with papers, knock them down," he
said. "It's okay as long as they don't touch me."
Before I left the car, Lennon pointed to the sleeping
wino leaning against the studio wall. He suggested the
guy could be disguised.*

*John hightailed it to the elevator when I signaled it
was clear, dragging me along with him. When the
elevator doors finally closed, he let out a nervous sigh
and somehow the ludicrousness of the morning dawned
on him. He burst out laughing. "I feel like I'm back in
Hard Day's Night or Help!" he said.*

*We used the three hours to talk, sipping tea as we
bounced from subject to subject. Before the interview
had begun, I had anticipated there would be subjects
difficult to broach, but John assuaged all fears by
responding openly with concern about everything. The
reference to Don Juan led to discussions about spiritual
searching led to discussions about psychedelics led to
discussions about specific drugs.*

PLAYBOY: Do you still take LSD?
LENNON: Not in years. A little mushroom or peyote
is not beyond my scope, you know, maybe twice a year
or something. But acid is a chemical. People are taking
it, though, even though you don't hear about it anymore. But people are still visiting the cosmos. It's just
that nobody talks about it; you get sent to prison.

We must always remember to thank the CIA and the
army for LSD, by the way. That's what people forget.
Everything is the opposite of what it is, isn't it? They

brought out LSD to control people, and what they did was give us freedom. Sometimes it works in mysterious ways its wonders to perform. But it sure as hell performs them.

If you look at the government report book on acid, the only ones who jumped out of the windows because of it were the ones in the army. I never knew anybody who jumped out of a window or killed themselves because of it. Let's face it, even Art Linkletter's daughter wasn't on acid when she jumped out of a window; it happened to her years later.

PLAYBOY: A flashback?

LENNON: I've never met anybody who's had a flashback. I've never had a flashback in my life and I took millions of trips in the Sixties, and I've never met anybody who had any problem. I've had bad trips and other people have had bad trips, but I've had a bad trip in real life. I've had a bad trip on a joint. I can get paranoid just sitting in a restaurant. I don't have to take anything.

Acid is only real life in CinemaScope. Whatever experience you had is what you would have had anyway. I'm not promoting, all you committees out there, and I don't use it because it's chemical, but all the garbage about what it did to people is garbage.

PLAYBOY: How about other drugs?

LENNON: If somebody gives me a joint, I might smoke it, but I don't go after it.

PLAYBOY: Cocaine?

LENNON: I had lots of it in my day, but I don't like it. It's a dumb drug. Your whole concentration goes on getting the next fix. I find caffeine easier to deal with. [*Ono enters*]

PLAYBOY: Do you drink much these days?

LENNON: No, I've had more than my share.

ONO: If we felt like drinking, we probably should; but, you see, we're not suppressing ourselves now, so we really feel no need for it.

PLAYBOY: What does your diet include besides sashimi and sushi, Hershey bars and cappuccinos?

LENNON: We're mostly macrobiotic, but sometimes I bring the family out for a pizza.

ONO: Intuition tells you what to eat. It's dangerous to try to unify things. Everybody has different needs. We went through vegetarianism and macrobiotic, but now, because we're in the studio, we do eat some junk food. We're trying to stick to macrobiotic: fish and rice and whole grains. You balance foods and eat foods indigenous to the area. Corn is the grain from this area.

PLAYBOY: And you both smoke up a storm.

LENNON: Macrobiotic people don't believe in the big C. Whether you take that as a rationalization or not, macrobiotics don't believe that smoking is bad for you. If we die, we're wrong.

We don't buy the establishment version of it at all. Nor do I think we came from monkeys, by the way.

PLAYBOY: To change the subject.

LENNON: To change the subject. That's another piece of garbage. What the hell's it based on? We couldn't've come from anything—fish, maybe, but not monkeys. I don't believe in the evolution of fish to monkeys to men. Why aren't monkeys changing into men now? It's absolute garbage. It's absolutely irrational garbage, as mad as the ones who believe the world was made only four thousand years ago, the fundamentalists. That and the monkey thing are both as insane as the other. I've nothing to base it on; it's only a gut feeling. They always draw that progression—these apes standing up suddenly. The early men are always drawn like apes, right? Because that fits in the theory we have been living with since Darwin.

I don't buy that monkey business. [*Singing*] "Too much monkey business . . ." [*Laughing*] I don't buy it. I've got no basis for it and no theory to offer, I just don't buy it. Something other than that. Something simpler. I don't buy anything other than "It always was and ever shall be." I can't conceive of anything less or more. The other theories change all the time. They set up these idols and then they knock them down. It keeps all the old professors happy in the university. It gives them something to do. I don't know if there's any harm in it except they ram it down everybody's throat. Everything they told me as a kid has already been disproved by the same type of "experts" who made them up in the first place. There.

17

Another week of days and nights with the Lennons passed. Double Fantasy *was nearing completion as each new layer of sound was added, whether "oohs" and "ahhs" and "over and over and over and woo" by the hired background singers, John and Yoko's own lead and backing vocals, or the musical instruments. One day, producer Douglas brought in a dulcimer player he had passed that day in Central Park. John sat in the booth as the player delivered his three notes until John was pleased. The musician was thrilled with the money he was paid and, merely as an afterthought, asked Jack whose album he was playing on. Jack pointed to John, sitting behind the glass. A bit later, the guy asked Jack the name of the man behind the glass. Jack responded, "John." As the man left with his dulcimer tucked under his arm, he turned to Jack once more to ask "John's" last name. "Lennon," he was told. The man left without changing expressions. In the middle of the next session, the door buzzer rang. The man with the dulcimer was back. He asked to speak to Jack. "Did I just play on John Lennon's album?" the guy asked. Jack smiled. "Yes," he said. The guy shook his head and wandered away utterly amazed.*

That night when I arrived to meet John at the apartment, he answered the door singing his greeting: "Here's David Sheff, come to ask questions with answers that no one will hear." He was singing to the tune of "Eleanor Rigby."

In the kitchen, the radio blurted a news report about a demonstration outside New York City against nuclear power. That veered our conversation to the political movements of today.

LENNON: All the "movements" got it all wrong. All the money and energy spent on attacking the nuclear industry is giving power to the nuclear industry. If the same energy and money was put into finding alternatives, they might get somewhere. While their minds are on the nuclear industry, there is no alternative, and what they want is unrealistic. As I said, they give it power. If they really want to deal with the problem, they have to take all the attention *off* it and *onto* the solution.

ONO: That's the secret of energy and the secret of life, in a way. It's like the three pots with seeds in them. One was watered with love, one was watered with hatred, and one was watered without love and without hatred, without any energy. Which one do you think survived the most? The ones with love and hatred survived the same. No matter what kind of energy you give it, it thrives. The one with no energy died, but love and hatred survived the same.

You see, when all that hate energy was focused on me, it was transformed into a fantastic energy. It was supporting me. If you are centered and you can transform all this energy that comes in, it will help you. If you believe it is going to kill you, it will kill you. The nuclear industry can take that hate energy as well as the other kind. So you must transform the energy into positive energy, in other directions, and the alternatives will come about. It's energy. Sheer energy.

LENNON [*singing, as in the TV commercial*]: Sheer en-er-gy . . .

ONO: We used to have that argument with Abbie [Hoffman] and Jerry [Rubin]. We don't believe in violence now and we didn't believe in violence then.

LENNON: Yeah, it was "We'll help with the concert, we'll sing our part." We were naïve, as well, thinking none of the money would go to anything nasty. Anyway, we had these incredible dialogues with Abbie. "We're not *against* that. We're *for* this."

The infamous San Diego meeting that got us into all the immigration problems was really a nonexistent situation. There was this so-called meeting with Jerry, Abbie, Allen Ginsberg, John Sinclair, John and Yoko, where they were trying to get us to go to the San Diego Republican Convention. When they described their plans, we just kept looking at each other. It was the poets and the straight politicals divided. Ginsberg was with us. He kept saying, "What are we trying to do, create another Chicago?" That's what they wanted. We said, "We ain't buying this. We're not going to draw children into a situation to create violence—so you can overthrow *what?*—and replace it with *what?*"

But then the story went out that we *were* going to San Diego. That was enough to get Immigration on us. They started attacking us through the Immigration Department, trying to throw us out of the country. But it was all based on this illusion, that you can create violence and overthrow what is and get communism or get some right-wing lunatic or a left-wing lunatic. They're all lunatics.

ONO: All the gun people telling us how to get peace: "You're always saying peace and love. You're just naïve. We have this strategy and we have to fight them like they fight us."

LENNON: And by the way, you [*to Yoko*] were the only woman there. We used to ask, "Are there women in this movement? Where is Mrs. Hoffman? Or your

THE **PLAYBOY** INTERVIEWS WITH
JOHN LENNON AND
YOKO ONO

John at the Playboy interview.

Newly named members of the Most Excellent Order of the British Empire (M.B.E.), the Beatles pose at the press conference in 1965.

Ringo and John on their way to North Wales to hear Maharishi Mahesh Yogi in 1967.

John on the eve of the release of *Magical Mystery Tour,* June 1967.

Above, John sports a shawl on his way to a meditation session with the Maharishi Mahesh Yogi in New Delhi, India, 1968.

John, not yet 30, married the 34-year-old Yoko Ono in Gibraltar on March 21, 1969.

1965

1965

1968

1969

1969

1970

1973

1980

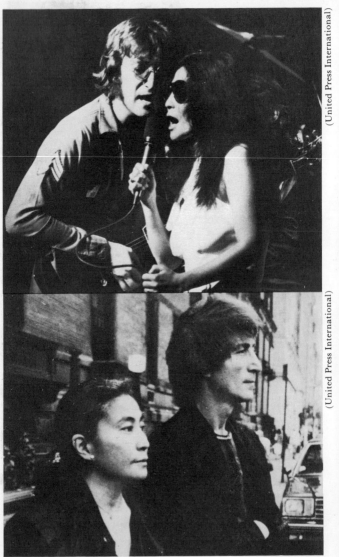

(United Press International)

(United Press International)

Top, John and Yoko in concert at Madison Square Garden to raise money for retarded children, August 1972. *Bottom,* John and Yoko on the street in front of their apartment house, the Dakota, the summer before he was shot.

Top, John at the "Hit Factory" studio in New York City where *Double Fantasy* was recorded. *Bottom,* John, Yoko, and the *Double Fantasy* recording team in the fall of 1980.

John and Yoko at the Playboy interview, September 1980.

lady friend? Where are they?" And they would say, "Oh, they're doing the typing back in the office."

ONO: Or "taking care of the baby."

LENNON: Or "taking care of the communal babies." They would never answer us, "Well, there is a great woman down in Chicago organizing the women," or anything.

PLAYBOY: What happened?

LENNON: What happened was there was no concert, 'cause we said: No way. To create Chicago is to create death and destruction. Apart from not being dumb enough to want to get hurt ourselves, we weren't going to create a riot or be responsible in any way. *No way*.

PLAYBOY: Then what happened with Immigration?

LENNON: Jerry couldn't keep his damn mouth shut, as usual. He was already on the press, blabbing off. Jerry told *Rolling Stone* there was going to be a San Diego concert with John and Yoko and their friends. Even though we had no plan of going to San Diego, the Right must have been looking and said, "Anyone who seems to be powerful enough to be used by these crazy radicals is dangerous, so therefore, why have them here? They are foreigners. We don't need any more freaks. We got enough of our own."

I understand their feeling precisely. I don't agree with them, but I understand where they are coming from. So anyway, we learned a big lesson from the Left and the Middle and the Right during that period. That was our education in politics.

PLAYBOY: What do you feel about Hoffman's re-emergence after being underground so long?

LENNON: Well, he got what he wanted, which is to be a sort of underground hero for anybody who still worships that manifestation of the underground. And he's got a book out of it. I don't know what I feel about it, because I don't feel that much about that period as a whole. It's like I'm kind of surprised to see Nixon on TV and I'm kind of surprised to see Abbie or Jerry on

TV. Maybe people get that when they see me or us. I feel, What are they doing there? Is this an old newsreel?

Anyway, all the preaching and moaning about *the bomb* and the apocalypse is really wishing for it. They think it's insoluble: The air is dirty, the food is crap, we don't have the president we want, therefore let's bomb ourselves. That's what they're really saying. "Let's have a nuclear confrontation and get it over with." But I don't want to get it over with. They're talking about what it's gonna be like when we bomb each other— burying their rice and their machine guns. It's a joke. Who wants to survive it? If it's gonna be, drop it right on the Dakota—

ONO: Wait a minute!

LENNON: I don't want to be around with skin falling off and those guys stockpiling weapons chasing everybody up the street. I just want to get there: BOOM— ashes to ashes.

ONO: Well, it won't happen.

LENNON: I know it won't happen.

ONO: I don't want to criticize their way because karmically—they have their own karma to sort out. When you think about the Sixties, though, and the people who were doing *something*, the things that we did really stopped the Vietnam War. There were some positive things that happened from that, and the Sixties was valid in that sense. There is a lot to criticize about that time, but still we are better that it happened. We are wiser for it. Everything has changed since then. We are all different. The cells in our body change totally every seven years or whatever. We're different people coping with a totally different situation now.

LENNON: Only the cells have changed to protect the innocent. [*Laughing*]

ONO: What world leaders don't understand when they say "We should do this," or whatever, is that they are working out their own karma. There might be a need in some of them to be violent, but you can't push it on other people. People should trust their own instincts.

LENNON: Well, there are the poor ones that didn't follow their instincts and went to Vietnam and got killed, crippled, and deformed and only woke up afterwards. That's the responsibility of the people that not only sent them there but sent them there under an illusion.

PLAYBOY: Explain what you mean about a leader being violent because of his own karma.

ONO: Each person has their own karma, even on the level of nonviolence. They need to be nonviolent because of their parents, or whatever.

LENNON: Mahatma Gandhi and Martin Luther King are great examples of fantastic nonviolents who died violently. I can never work that out. We're pacifists, but I'm not sure what it means when you're such a pacifist that you get shot. I can never understand that.

ONO: As Harry Nilsson says, "Everything is the opposite of what it is, isn't it?"

LENNON: Isn't it?

ONO: I mean maybe John and I have needs to be peaceniks because we're—

LENNON: Because we're so violent.

ONO: Maybe we have so much violence in us that we suppress it. Gandhi's trip was because of Gandhi, but maybe if someone wants to do what Gandhi did, it might not work for them. It's the same about the Western man's illusion about Christ. If you follow Jesus exactly, you are going to be on the cross. For somebody who is not on the cross—in a conceptual, symbolic sense—you will always feel guilty that somehow you are not on it. The whole masochism is created by the cross image.

LENNON: So anyway, they're always talking about the details of how many would survive and would there be more Chinese restaurants or Italian restaurants after the bomb? Will we be listening to the balalaika or the sitar? It's nonsense. It's placing all attention on the bomb and weapons. Focusing on the nuclear industry will help the nuclear industry. Focusing on *1984* will make *1984* a reality.

18

Talk about politics and the Sixties eventually led to the name of Bob Dylan, a peer of sorts of John's. "Is it distressing," I asked, "to see Dylan, once a fellow cynic, a born-again Christian?"

LENNON: I don't like to comment on it. For whatever reason he's doing it, it's personal for him and he needs to do it. I'm not distressed by the fact that Dylan is doing what Dylan wants or needs to do. I like him personally. I've known him for years, though I haven't seen him in years. I understand it and have nothing against it or for it. If he needs it, let him do it.

PLAYBOY: Isn't Dylan preaching, though?

LENNON: People who don't want to hear it will just leave the theater.

PLAYBOY: Will they? It's back to the responsibility thing. People stay in the theater because he's Bob Dylan.

LENNON: Well, anybody who wants to hear Dylan just because of who he is isn't gonna understand what Dylan is saying now or then. They're just following some kind of image. They're the sheep anyway. Still, the whole religion business does suffer from the "Onward Christian Soldiers" bit. There's too much talk about soldiers and marching and converting. I'm not pushing Buddhism, because I'm no more a Buddhist than I am a Christian, but there's one thing I admire about the religion: There is no proselytizing.

ONO: Each person in the world has a song in his heart. They should listen to that.

LENNON: I was brought up Christian and I only now understand some of the things that Christ was saying in those parables anyway—when I got away from the interpretations that were thrown at me all my life. There is more to it. But I must say I was surprised when old Bobby boy did go that way. I was very surprised. But I was also surprised when he went to that Jewish group. That surprised me, too, because all I ever hear whenever I hear about him is—and people can quote me and make *me* feel silly, too—but all I ever think of is "Don't follow leaders, watch the parking meters." It's the same man, but it isn't the same man, and I don't want to say anything about a man who is searching or has found it. It is unfortunate when people say, "This is the only way." That's the only thing I've got against anybody, if they are saying, "This is the only answer." I don't want to hear about that. There isn't one answer to anything.

But I understand it. I understand him completely, how he got in there, because I've been frightened enough myself to want to latch on to *something*. It's that wanting to belong. It sounds like an excuse for stupidity half the time, but it's a dual thing one has of wanting to be outside of society because one can see through it, as it were, and it allows the clarity of vision for an artist or poet to look at society separately, but at the same time wanting desperately to be accepted by society, too. To *belong*. I'm like the monkey in the Chinese story. I'm a bit quicker in and a bit quicker out. I jump in because I want to belong and I jump out because I remember the real game is not to belong but to belong to the whole thing, not to one little section of it.

Offhand, one can talk about Dylan's traumatic divorce from Sarah and the separation from his children; first of all, feeling like a lot of husbands away for the weekend—"Oh, I'm free again, I'm a bachelor again; I get to do all the little things I couldn't do when I was a father"—and then finding out that that wasn't where it was at, finding that he missed his family. Instead of having a motorcycle accident to knock him out, which is what he did the first time, he latched on to this. What he needs is to go away and do what he did without smashing himself on a motorbike, to get away from the sycophants whether they be Jesus sycophants or JDL sycophants.

PLAYBOY: Perhaps he simply became disillusioned with politics?

LENNON: Well, he wasn't ever that political, really. He wrote "Blowin' in the Wind" and "Soldier Song," but they're just poetic politics, folk music of the day. He's commenting on what's going on, like a journalist. He never stood in the corner and shouted anything. It's what people read into what he did. It's only the constant necessity to identify and label people for the media and public. Maybe millions of people have been born again and then next Friday forgotten all about it. It just so happens that Dylan did it in public.

ONO: I never had the adulation for him, so I was never disappointed when Dylan went that way. He's simply relying on some system.

LENNON: Yoko was never under any Dylan mystique. She never thought much of him either way.

PLAYBOY: What about you, John?

LENNON: For a period I was very impressed with him. But I stopped listening to Dylan with both ears after "Highway 64" [*sic*] and "Blonde on Blonde," and even then it was because George would sit down and make me listen.

PLAYBOY: That was "61."

LENNON: I don't know what year it was.

PLAYBOY: No, "Highway 61." You took the wrong route. [*Laughter*]

LENNON: So much for my memory. Anyway, I was never a fan. Of anything. I stopped being a fan when I started doin' it myself. When I was a kid I was a fan of Elvis and Little Richard and Chuck Berry. I still have a soft spot for them.

You have to think in terms of process. Relying on

your own spirit is healthy. If Dylan is into Jesus because of needing to belong, whatever, perhaps the next step will be to see the good of the experience as well as the other side.

19

PLAYBOY: Dylan went to Christ, but what about the period when you both became devotees of Arthur Janov's primal-scream therapy?

LENNON: We ain't devotees of nothing.

PLAYBOY: But you went through primal-scream therapy?

LENNON: In the early Seventies, Janov's book came in the mail and the name, *Primal Scream,* intrigued me. I mean Yoko's been screaming a long time. Just the words, the title, made my heart flutter. Then I read the testimonials—you know, "I am Charlie so-and-so, I went in and this is what happened to me." I thought, That's me, that's me. It was the early days together and we were living in Ascot and there was still a lot of shit coming down on us. And these people say they get to this thing and they scream and they feel better. Okay, it's something other than taking a tab of acid and feeling better, so I thought, let's try it.

PLAYBOY: What was the therapy like?

LENNON: They do this thing where they mess around with you until you reach a point where you hit this scream thing. You go with it—they encourage you to go with it—and you kind of make a physical, mental, cosmic breakthrough with the scream itself. I can compare it to acid inasmuch as you take the trip, and what you do with it afterwards when the drug's worn off is what you do with it afterwards when the drug's worn off. But there's no taking away from the initial scream. That's what you go for.

ONO: It's especially for men.

LENNON: Oh, poor men again.

ONO: Because they never have the chance to cry because they're always told not to cry or scream or show emotion like that. I wasn't very impressed with it.

LENNON: She came along for the ride. I was the male who had never cried, you know. She could cry. My defenses were so great. I mean the cocky chip-on-the-shoulder, macho, aggressive rock 'n' roll hero who knew all the answers and the smart quip, the sharp-talking king of the world, was actually a terrified guy who didn't know how to cry. Simple. Now I can cry. That's what I learned from primal therapy. We were there six months. We had a nice house in L.A. We'd go down to the session, have a good cry, and come back and swim in the pool. And you'd always feel like after acid or a good joint, you know, sort of in the pool tingling and everything was fine. But then your defenses would all come up again—like the acid would wear off, the joint would wear off—and you'd go back for another fix.

PLAYBOY: When was this?

LENNON: I don't know the year. Name the record. *Plastic Ono?*

ONO: Yeah, '69 to '70. John got through the angry-young-man thing. You know the urge to cry exists in men, but they transform it to anger, which is more acceptable. But women have anger, too. We transform it into the more acceptable form of crying—or silence.

LENNON: Yeah, and breast cancer.

PLAYBOY: Do you still take that therapy?

LENNON: Are you kidding? No, I'm not that stupid. The secret is to learn how to cry. Once you know how to do it, you know. I don't believe all the garbage about going back and back and keep digging and digging and digging.

PLAYBOY: Isn't it billed as an alternative to psychotherapy?

LENNON: I would never have gone to psychotherapy. I would never have gone if there hadn't been this promise of this scream, this liberating scream. And it was fantastic. Yoko never needed it. She did her own primal on stage.

ONO: And I wasn't looking for a daddy.

PLAYBOY: A daddy?

ONO: I think Janov was a daddy for John. I think he has this father complex and he's always searching for a daddy.

PLAYBOY: Would you explain?

ONO: I had a daddy, a real daddy, sort of a big and strong father like a Billy Graham. But growing up, I saw his other side—his weak side. I saw the hypocrisy. So whenever I see something that is *supposed* to be so big and wonderful—a guru or primal scream—I'm very cynical.

LENNON: She fought with Janov all the time. He couldn't deal with it.

ONO: I'm not searching for the big daddy. I look for something else in men—something that is tender and weak and I feel like I want to help.

LENNON: Yeah, and I'm the lucky cripple she chose!

ONO: I have this mother instinct, whatever. But I was not hung up on finding a father, because I had one who disillusioned me. John never had a chance to get disillusioned about his father since his father wasn't around. People in general are so frantic about daddies because they're the ones that are never home and they never got enough of daddy. Somehow there is a distance about them, a mystique. That explains the adoration and yearning for daddy, whereas mommy was always there at home.

PLAYBOY: Do you agree with that assessment, John?

LENNON: A lot of us are looking for fathers. Mine was physically not there. Most people's are not there *mentally* and physically, like always at the office or busy with other things. So all these leaders, parking meters, are all substitute fathers, whether they be religious or political. . . . All this bit about electing a president! We pick our own daddy out of a dog pound of daddies. This is the daddy that looks like the daddy in the commercials. He's got the nice gray hair and the right teeth and the parting's on the right side. Okay? This is the daddy we choose. The dog pound of daddies, which is the political arena, gives us a president. Then we put him on a platform and start punishing him and screaming at him because daddy can't do miracles: Daddy doesn't heal us; we don't feel better. So then we move the daddy out in four years and we get a new daddy.

PLAYBOY: So Janov was a daddy for you. Who else?

ONO: Before, there was Maharishi.

LENNON: Maharishi was a father figure, Elvis Presley might have been a father figure. I don't know. Robert Mitchum. Any male image is a father figure. There's nothing that wrong with it until you give them the right to give you a sort of recipe for your life. What happens is somebody comes along with a good piece of truth. Instead of the truth being looked at, the person who brought it is looked at. It's like when bad news comes, they shoot the messenger. When the good news comes, they worship the messenger and they don't listen to the message. Have you ever met a Christian who behaves like a Christian? Or in the other religions, have you met a person of the faith who behaves like the ideal? Well, nobody's perfect, right? Nobody's perfect, et cetera, et cetera, except for all these people who are *named* as being perfect.

The same thing happens in something like primal therapy. Arthur Janov accidentally discovered his thing. Before that, he's a straight Freudian psychologist. He finds this screaming by accident and now he's writing theories, books, God knows what about it. If Janov's thing ever got as big as Christianity and then he died, they're going to be worshiping Janov. Not to take away from Janov's or Werner Erhard's or whoever's system or method of learning to swim. The swimming's fine. It's with the Beatles, too. The Beatles are not Jesus are not Janov are not Erhard. Maybe they had a nice way of swimming, but the swimming is the point. [*Excitedly*] The records are the point. Not the Beatles as individuals!

ONO: I don't think so. I think the Beatles—

LENNON: Oh, Jesus! [*Laughing, he screams and jumps up.*] I thought I *finally* cleared it all up. Oh, shit!

ONO: The essence of what they were communicating in music wouldn't happen with the world. It was that the whole package—

LENNON: But that is not the point. Christ's package had the Virgin Mary and the miracles and going into the desert. Buddha had his whole package. But still the bare bones of the message is very similar to the Marxist message. Whether it be Christianity, Muhammadanism, Buddhism, Confucianism, Marxism, Maoism, everything. They're all about the person and not what the person said.

ONO: All the isms are daddies.

LENNON: This ism, that ism. Ism, ism, ism. It's always some big guy in the sky. And if they're dead, that's really good.

ONO: People like to personalize things. People personalize God. People picture God as an old man with a beard.

LENNON: They don't know it's an old woman with a beard. [*Chuckles*] It's easier to identify with a human than with a concept. The Muhammadans tried it by not allowing images. There's a little of that in the Christian church; the agnostics, meaning self-knowledge, were the true essence of Christianity, but they were stamped out or chased to the hills. The agnostic tradition is similar to the Zen Buddhists, which is not quite Buddhism. There are also the Sufis in Moslem. There's always one group that says ''Self, self, self'': Here's a set of rules to enlighten the self and it *just so happens* to come by this mailgram. Read Christ's words, read Bud-

dha's words, any of the great words. But we don't need the imagery and the "Thou must worship like me or die." People got the image I was anti-Christ or antireligion. I'm not at all. I'm a most religious fellow. I'm religious in the sense of—
ONO: Religious in the sense of admitting there is—
LENNON: —more to it than meets the eye. I'm certainly not an atheist. There is more that we still could know. I think this magic is just a way of saying science we don't know yet or we haven't explored yet. That's not antireligious at all.

20

PLAYBOY: John, are you still looking for a daddy?
LENNON: No. You see, I learned to cry, not through primal therapy but through living with Yoko. She'd say, "Do you want another daddy? Okay, we'll go and visit one." "You want another daddy? We'll visit another one." Until I turned around and said, "Okay, enough with the daddies." You see, they always show themselves. When we get around them, because we're famous, the daddies blow their cool because they can't contain their eagerness for power and glory. It showed itself in Maharishi; it showed itself in Janov, who suddenly came on like a silver-haired Jeff Chandler, impressed with our celebrity.
ONO: One day he brought cameras into the room. We walked out.
LENNON: Even under a daddy I'm not going to be filmed, especially rolling around the floor screaming. So then he started to berate us: "Some people are so big they won't be filmed." He said he just happened to be filming that session. "Who are you kidding, Mr. Janov?"

He just happened to be filming the session with John and Yoko in it.

At first I was bitter about Maharishi being human and bitter about Janov being human. Well, I'm not bitter anymore. They're human and I'm only thinking what a dummy I was, you know. Although I meditate and I cry.

ONO: It's sad that society is structured in such a way that people cannot really open up to each other and therefore they need a certain theater to go to cry, or something like that.

LENNON: Well, you went to *est*.

ONO: Yes, I wanted to check it out.

LENNON: We went to Janov for the same reason.

ONO: But *est* people are given a reminder—

LENNON: Yeah, but I wouldn't go and sit in a room and not pee.

ONO: Well, *you* did in primal scream.

LENNON: Oh, but I had you with me.

ONO: Anyway, when I went to *est* I saw Werner Erhard—the same thing! He's a nice showman and he's got a nice gig there. I felt the same thing when we went to Sai Baba in India. In India you have to be a guru instead of a pop star. . . . Guru is the pop star of India, and pop star is the guru here.

LENNON: But as I was saying earlier, this doesn't mean there isn't validity in the message. The swimming may be fine, right? But forget about the teacher. If the Beatles had a message, it was that. With the Beatles, the music is the point. Not the Beatles as individuals. The early Elvis records live on without Elvis being a beautiful male animal who swung his pelvis. As I said, I didn't see him. I heard the music first. Afterwards I saw that it did come in a package. But *you don't need the package*. With Elvis, the basic thing, the basic energy, is on the records. Just like you don't need the Christian package or the Marxist package or the Buddhist package to get the message. It's easier to identify with the package than with the message—and then you miss it completely. Forget about the teacher. Learn to swim.

PLAYBOY: And the Beatles taught people how to swim?

LENNON: If the Beatles or the Sixties had a message, it was to learn to swim. Period. And once you learn to swim, swim. The people who are hung up on the Beatles and the Sixties dream missed the whole point when the Beatles and the Sixties *became* the point. Carrying the Beatles or the Sixties dream around all your life is like carrying the Second World War and Glenn Miller around. That's not to say you can't enjoy Glenn Miller or the Beatles, but to live in that dream is the twilight zone. It's not living now. It's an illusion.

PLAYBOY: What is "now" for you?

ONO: John has talked about the Sixties and how it gave us a taste for freedom—sexual and otherwise. It was like an orgy. Then, after that big come that we had together, men and women somehow lost track of each other and a lot of families and relationships split apart. I really think that what happened in the Seventies can be compared to what happened under Nazism with Jewish families. Only the force that split them in the Seventies came from the inside, not from the outside. We tried to rationalize it as the price we were paying for our freedom. And John is saying in his new song, "Starting Over," OK, we had the energy in the Sixties, in the Seventies we separated, but let's start over in the Eighties. John's song makes me feel like crying. He's reaching out to me, reaching out after all that's happened. He's reaching out over the battlefield of dead families even though it's more difficult this time around.

It's like what I'm saying in "Kiss Kiss Kiss." There is the sound of a woman coming to a climax on it, and she is crying out to be held, to be touched. It will be controversial, because people will feel it's less natural to hear the sounds of a woman's lovemaking than, say, the sound of a Concorde, killing the atmosphere and polluting nature. But the lovemaking is the sound that will make us survive. You see, I believe we will blossom in the Eighties. I believe it. It's hard to see, but we will. I'm not talking about in terms of capitalism or materialism so much as spiritually. Our spirit will rise, especially when there's meagerness around us on a material level. The spirit will rise. We can't rely on this system.

The Seventies, unlike what people think, was a marvelous age, leading to the hope I feel. A lot of things happened, though on the surface it didn't look like it. John and I were almost like a symbol of what happened in the Seventies. We were sitting, but inside us there was a big revolution. We were cleaning up and tuning in psychically.

People criticize the "Me Decade," but if you tune in to yourself you might find yourself. And then you might find other people, too. Before the Sixties, we were not allowed to tune in to ourselves. We saw only form. No substance. So it's all a natural progression to the Eighties. It will be a marvelous age. We're going to be closer together. We don't have to paint our faces like we did in the Sixties. We don't have to do that anymore. But inside there will be true liberation. If we don't liberate ourselves, it's 1984. We're going to do it. I *feel* it. It will be beautiful.

PLAYBOY: What is the Eighties dream to you, John?

LENNON: Well, you make your own dream. That's the Beatles story, isn't it? That's Yoko's story. That's what I'm saying now. Produce your own dream. If you want to save Peru, go save Peru. It's quite possible to do anything, but not if you put it on the leaders and the parking meters. Don't expect Carter or Reagan or John Lennon or Yoko Ono or Bob Dylan or Jesus Christ to come and do it for you. You have to do it yourself.

That's what the great masters and mistresses have been saying ever since time began. They can point the way, leave signposts and little instructions in various books that are now called holy and worshiped for the cover of the book and not what it says, but the instructions are all there for all to see, have always been and always will be. There's nothing new under the sun. All the roads lead to Rome. And people cannot provide it for you. I can't wake you up. *You* can wake you up. I can't cure you. *You* can cure you.

PLAYBOY: What is it that keeps people from accepting that message?

LENNON: It's fear of the unknown. The unknown is what it is. And to be frightened of it is what sends everybody scurrying around in circles chasing dreams, illusions, wars, peace, love, hate, all that—it's all illusion. Unknown is what it is. Accept that it's unknown and it's plain sailing. Everything is unknown—then you're ahead of the game. That's what it is. Right?

PLAYBOY: You're optimistic?

LENNON: I am. And I'm not the only one. Maybe the ones preaching the negative future get all the press, but there are others. Walk through the park and there are people holding hands and kissing. New York is beginning to look like Paris when I was younger, when I was twenty-four and people were holding hands and kissing under bridges. It's happening again. People are dreaming again.

PLAYBOY: It seems to be working for you.

ONO: It's like a duet, you know. It's a very good combination.

LENNON: A *very* good combination.

PART THREE

21

On September 29, Newsweek *magazine carried a two-page interview with John and Yoko. Yoko had told us there would be an item on their return to public life in* Newsweek, *but the piece, released on the wire services, was fairly substantial. Although the material we had was far more in-depth, Barry Golson and I were somewhat discouraged at having been scooped. We decided to ask John and Yoko about it.*

We taxied uptown to the Dakota, where the usual knot of fans was gathered. Inside the Studio One offices, we were joined by free-lance photographer Tom Zuk. We had almost forgotten it was the day we had scheduled for photographs.

In the outer office, John was sprawled in an armchair, tying his sneaker laces. "Heyyy," he said cheerily, "tits 'n' ass!"

Barry, assuming he was being greeted in his official capacity, responded in kind. Waving an open copy of Newsweek *he had with him, he said, "John, you rat. You blew our exclusive."*

John looked up from the chair. "Yeah, Yoko and I talked a bit with the Newsweek *reporter. For the album, you know. Notice their trick: It was to be an interview with both of us, but get this." He read from the introduction. " 'Recently Lennon and Ono sat down with* Newsweek's *Barbara Graustark for his first major interview in five years.' Pretty crafty, huh! 'For his . . .' So anyway, guess I don't know when to shut up, do I?" He stood up and put his hands on his hips. "Well, what can I do to make it up to you boys?"*

Barry's mind worked quickly. "Just the other day we

were fantasizing about what it would have been like to ask one of the great composers—Beethoven, for instance— how he came to write his symphonies." We all laughed at the obvious flattery. "John, have you ever gone over all your music, song by song, to recall who wrote what, and under what circumstances, and what memories the songs might inspire?"

Surprisingly, John's response was immediate and enthusiastic. "Are you kidding?" he said. "Instead of talking about Beatles reunions and all that rubbish? I'm proud of my work. I'll give you the definitive version, the whole damned thing—at least my version. On this sort of thing, I have a terrific memory. You can do it from the womb to the grave. Boom!"

The three of us chatted with the tape recorders going as we moved into the inner office where Yoko was waiting and photographer Zuk was setting up his equipment. The conversation, which proved a fruitful one, went on through the clicking of the camera.

LENNON: I hope you don't think we blew our jism with *Newsweek,* because I don't think we did. This is larger and better and deeper. It will be *the* reference book.

PLAYBOY: Well, you'll probably only have to do it once in your life.

LENNON: Yeah, in my life!

PLAYBOY: Before you start in on it—

LENNON: The Beatles memory-lane bit, you mean.

PLAYBOY: Yes, while we get through with the photos, how did you and Paul work together as composers? There are a lot of versions of what actually went on.

LENNON: Well . . . take "Michelle," one of Paul's songs. He and I were staying somewhere and he walked in and hummed the first few bars, with the words, you ˈ——— ings verse of "Michelle"], and he says, "Where ɔ from here?" I had been listening to [blues Nina Simone—I think it was "I Put a Spell on There was a line in it that went [*taps his fingers* *and sings, gruffly*]: "I love *you,* I love *you,* I love *you.*" That's what made me think of the middle eight for "Michelle": [*sings*] "I *love* you, I *love* you, I *l-o-ove* you."

So . . . my contribution to Paul's songs was always to add a little bluesy edge to them. Otherwise, y'know, "Michelle" is a straight ballad, right? He provided a lightness, an optimism, while I would always go for the sadness, the discords, the bluesy notes. There was a period when I thought I didn't write melodies, that Paul wrote those and I just wrote straight, shouting rock 'n' roll. But of course, when I think of some of my own songs—"In My Life," or some of the early stuff, "This Boy"—I was writing melody with the best of them.

PLAYBOY: Paul had more musical training than you did, right?

LENNON: Yeah, his father was a jazz musician. When I met him he could play guitar, trumpet, and piano. Doesn't mean to say he has a greater talent, but his musical education was better. I could only play the mouth organ and two chords on a guitar when we met. I tuned the guitar like a banjo. I'd learned guitar from my mother, who only knew how to play banjo, so my guitar only had five strings on it. Paul taught me how to play the guitar proper—but I had to learn the chords left-handed, because Paul is left-handed. So I learned them upside down and I'd go home and reverse them. I can still play upside down, with the high strings on top. That's what I was doing the day we met—playing on stage with a group, playing a five-string guitar like a banjo, when he was brought around from the audience to meet me. In the Hunter Davies biography of the Beatles, there's a photo of the day we met. [*Pause*] You see, I told you I have a good memory.

PLAYBOY: But you didn't compose your stuff separately, as other accounts have said?

LENNON: No, no, no. I said that, but I was lying [*laughs*]. By the time I said that, we were so sick of this idea of writing and singing together, especially me, that I started this thing about, "We never wrote together, we were never in the same room." Which wasn't true. We wrote a *lot* of stuff together, one-on-one, eyeball to eyeball. Like in "I Want to Hold Your Hand," I remember when we got the chord that made the song. We were in Jane Asher's house, downstairs in the cellar playing on the piano at the same time. And we had, "Oh you-u-u . . . got that something . . ." And Paul hits this chord and I turn to him and say, "That's *it!*" I said, "Do that again!" In those days, we really used to absolutely write like that—both playing into each other's noses. We spent hours and hours and hours . . . We wrote in the back of vans together. We wrote "She Loves You" in a van on the way to Newcastle. And "From Me to You."

PLAYBOY: Do you ever feel that you've missed him artistically, musically?

LENNON: No. I mean, we worked together partly because the demand on us was *tremendous*. They'd want a record, a single, every three months, and we'd do it in twelve hours in a hotel or a van. So the cooperation was functional as well as musical.

PLAYBOY: And you don't think that cooperation, that magic between you, is something you've missed in your work since?

LENNON: I never actually felt a loss. I don't want it to sound negative, like I didn't need Paul, because when he was there, obviously, it worked. But I can't—it's easier to say what my contribution was to him than what he gave to me. And he'd say the same.

PLAYBOY: What about the lyrics? How did you work together?

LENNON: You'd have to break down the songs, which we'll do. I always had an easier time with lyrics, although Paul is quite a capable lyricist—who doesn't think he is, therefore he doesn't try. He would avoid the problem rather than face it. But in the early days lyrics didn't really count as long as we had some vague theme: "She loves you, he loves her, and they love each other." It was the hook and the line and the sound we were going for. That's still my attitude, but . . . I can't leave lyrics alone; I have to make them make sense apart from the song.

PLAYBOY: When you say Paul doesn't think he's a good lyricist—

LENNON: I don't think he's made an effort to, but I don't think he's incapable. I don't think he's as good as *me,* but he's certainly not incapable. "Hey Jude" is a damn good set of lyrics and I made *no* contribution to that. A couple of lines he's come up with show indications he's a good lyricist, but he just never took it anywhere. He wrote the lyrics to "Yesterday." Although the lyrics don't resolve into any sense, they're *good* lines. They certainly work. You know what I mean? They're good—but if you read the whole song, it doesn't *say* anything; you don't know what happened. She left and he wishes it was yesterday—that much you get—but it doesn't really resolve. So, mine didn't used to resolve, either. . . .

PLAYBOY: But what about a complex song like "Eleanor Rigby"?

LENNON: Yeah, "Rigby." Ah, the first verse was his and the rest are basically mine. But the way he did it . . . Well, he knew he had a song. But by that time he didn't want to ask for my help, and we were sitting around with Mal Evans and Neil Aspenall, so he said to us, "Hey, you guys, finish up the lyrics."

Now I was there with Mal, a telephone installer who was our road manager, and Neil, who was a student accountant, and I was insulted and hurt that Paul had just thrown it out in the air. He actually meant he wanted *me* to do it, and of course there isn't a line of theirs in the song because I finally went off to a room with Paul and we finished the song. But that's how [*gestures*] . . . that's the kind of insensitivity he would have, which upset me in later years. That's the kind of person he is. "Here, finish these lyrics up," like to *anybody* who was around.

PLAYBOY: Would Paul envision a theme? "Rigby" was about loneliness. . . .

LENNON: Oh, he had the whole start: "Eleanor Rigby picks up the rice in the church where a wedding has been." What's the next line?

PLAYBOY: "Lives in a dream."

LENNON: Yeah, and he had the story and knew where it was going. So we had to work out, "Well, is there anybody else in this story?" We came up with Father McCartney for a bit, but Paul said his dad would be upset, so we made it into McKenzie, even though McCartney sounded better. And then we went on to new characters. . . . It's hard to describe, even with the clarity of memory, the moment the apple falls. The thing will start moving along at a speed of its own, then you wake up at the end of it and have this whole thing on paper, you know? Who said what to whom as we were writing, I don't know.

I do know that George Harrison was there when we came up with [*sings*] "Ah, look at all the lonely people." He and George were settling on that as I left the studio to go to the toilet, and I heard the lyric and turned around and said, "That's *it!*" The violins backing was Paul's idea. Jane Asher had turned him on to Vivaldi, and it was very good, the violins, straight out of Vivaldi. I can't take any credit for that, a-tall.

PLAYBOY: Speaking of falling apples and Newton, do you feel that that kind of creativity *does* ebb? Mathematicians, and some musicians, do their best work when they're young.

LENNON: Yeah, but . . . well, you put the fear of God into me, bringing up *that* bogeyman . . . but many people didn't start writing or painting until they were forty, fifty, and sixty. So there's hope yet.

PLAYBOY: But usually not musicians, right?

LENNON: Well, I don't know the history of musicians.

PLAYBOY: Mozart, for instance, whose great compositions cáme when he was very young—

LENNON: Oh, him. Well, it comes and goes. I can't believe it goes away forever . . . but you can never be twenty-four again. You can't be that hungry twice. That can never, never be.

PLAYBOY: But in the last ten years you've never wondered if it might not come as easily, as naturally again as it once did?

LENNON: Sure I have. I thought, Maybe that's *it*. Maybe music's over. I mean, I *was* preparing not to make any music again. . . . But as to that bogeyman, there's . . . here, I don't know if this will gel for you: When the Beatles played in America for the first time, they were already old hands. It was pure craftsmanship. The jism had gone out of the performance a long, long time ago. We had already done *half* the world—England and Europe—and by the time we got to America, it didn't have the guts. We were already out of creative performing by then. Only the excitement of the American kids, the American scene, made it come alive. It was a show we knew like that [*snaps fingers*].

But in the early days of performing, whether it was Hamburg or Liverpool, when we were still playing dance halls, there was still a lot of inspirational energy. We hadn't started repeating our little movements, our little licks. So in that respect, the Beatles' *live* creativity had gone long before they came to America. And in the same respect the creativity of songwriting had left Paul and me . . . well, by the mid-Sixties it had become a *craft*.

And *yet* . . . a different kind of thing comes in. It's like a love affair. When you first meet, you can have the hots twenty-four hours a day for each other. But after fifteen or twenty years, a different kind of sexual *and* intellectual relationship develops, right? It's still love, but it's different. So there's that kind of difference in creativity, too. As in a love affair, two creative people can destroy themselves trying to recapture that youthful spirit, at twenty-one or twenty-four, of creating without even being aware of how it's happening. One takes to drugs, to drinks, to knock oneself out. . . .

Like, I wrote *In His Own Write*, at least some of it, while I was still at school, and it came spontaneously. But I wrote *A Spaniard in the Works* with a bottle of Johnnie Walker. Once it became "We want another book from you, Mr. Lennon," I could only loosen up to it with a bottle of Johnnie Walker, and I thought, If it takes a bottle every night to get me to write . . . That's why I didn't write anymore.

PLAYBOY: You've never tried to write again, aside from music?

LENNON: I did, yeah. Actually, it was when I stopped music and started this househusband business. I got frantic during one period that I was supposed to be *creating* things, so I sat down and wrote about two hundred pages of mad stuff—*In His Own Write*-ish. It's there in a box, but it isn't right. Some of it's funny, but it's not right enough. You know, I always set out to write a children's book. I always wanted to write *Alice in Wonderland*. I think I still have that as a secret ambition. And I think I will do it when I'm older.

PLAYBOY: When you say the creativity went out of your relationship with Paul by the mid-Sixties, that's a little hard to believe. There are a lot of people who feel that the period between 1966 and 1970 was the most fertile musical period of all.

LENNON: It wasn't. Well, it was fertile in the way a relationship between a man and a woman becomes more fertile after eight or ten years. The *depth* of the Beatles' songwriting, or of John and Paul's contribution to the Beatles, in the late Sixties was more pronounced; it had a more mature, more intellectual—whatever you want to call it—approach. We were different. We were older. We knew each other on all kinds of levels that we didn't when we were teen-agers. The early stuff—the "Hard Day's Night" period, I call it—was the sexual equivalent of the beginning hysteria of a relationship.

And the "Sgt. Pepper–Abbey Road" period was the mature part of the relationship. And maybe, had we gone on together, maybe something interesting would have come of it. It wouldn't have been the same. But maybe it was a marriage that *had* to end. Some marriages don't get through that phase. It's hard to speculate about what would have been.

As the preceding conversation was taking place, largely between Lennon and Golson, I began to question Yoko alone in another part of the office. The photography session continued.

PLAYBOY: I wanted to talk more about your reactions to the way people speak about you, Yoko—that it was you who destroyed that relationship, who broke up the Beatles.

ONO: Well, my version is that I met an interesting guy and we got together, and suddenly he's got all these in-laws. I got along with each of them, meaning Paul, George, and Ringo, and none of them were nasty to me. They were pretty civilized about it. But the people around them . . . I mean, I heard there were plans to *kill* me.

PLAYBOY: Really?

ONO: But it had nothing to do with the Beatles themselves. They were very civilized and kind to me. They're intelligent and sensitive people, and as friends they understand me.

PLAYBOY: Then what about the statement of Paul's you quoted earlier: "Why does John have to spend *all* his time with her?"

ONO: Well, it's natural for men and women to spend a lot of time together initially. In our case, we still do . . . but still, it was a natural thing to do. But the Beatles were used to situations where they were closer to each other than to their women. And of course, I was not aware of that. But I don't think you could have broken up four very strong people like them, even if you tried. So there must have been something that happened within them—not an outside force at all.

PLAYBOY: How did you deal with the fact that many fans did feel that your relationship with John broke up the Beatles?

ONO: Well, fans expect us to be perfect, you know. And of course, we were not accommodating them. There was such a close inspection of our life, and, yes, it did affect us.

The picture session ended, and John joined Yoko on the couch.

ONO: We were talking about me splitting up the Beatles.

PLAYBOY: John's anger about the way people resented you has certainly come through in this interview. Do you feel the same way about the fans' reactions, Yoko?

ONO: No. [*Hesitates*] I feel amazed. I'm amazed that people can be so concerned about somebody else's life. I mean, what about their *own* lives?

PLAYBOY: Maybe that's why they're so concerned about someone else's life—because they can't deal with their own, or their own is simply boring.

ONO [*laughing*]: Well, their lives obviously should be more interesting to them. *Every* life is interesting. Every life can be a huge encyclopedia. There's not that much different between our lives and somebody else's. You can pick a person on a street and start asking questions, and you'll find that it's full of miracles. It's a pity somebody has to think his life is less interesting than ours, and put his mind onto our lives.

LENNON: You know Linda has taken the same kind of shellacking Yoko got and we have a deep sympathy for her because we know what she's been through. She got the same kind of insults, hatred, absolute garbage thrown at her for no reason whatsoever other than she fell in love with Paul McCartney. It's just a crying shame the way both Linda and Paul—uh, Linda and Yoko were treated. It's just a reflection of the state of the minds of people in the media who should know better. I mean, they're bloody educated people, aren't they? But they can be so narrow and petty and stupid. They were insulting them on such a *personal level*—about the way they look and things like that, that they would *never* do to anybody, man or woman, in person. I mean, how *dare* they? I mean, that fed the fires of the public who picked up that attitude. The attitude was absolutely created by the press—the females, too, in the press. Women are their own worst enemies a lot of the time. A lot of these women are still digging in.

22

PLAYBOY: Another thing I wanted to clear up about your role reversal: John as househusband, Yoko as businesswoman. Hasn't it really been a kind of game for you both, because you knew you could always go back, or stop?

ONO: Yes, it's true. I'm not a former housewife who never had anything—

LENNON: And I'm a housewife who also has a nanny and an assistant and a cook and a cleaner. I wasn't a poor strugglin' housewife who *had* to cook three meals a day. I cooked for fun.

ONO: And you had also achieved something in the world outside. Most housewives never had any achievements.

LENNON: Yes, right, right. I couldn't say I gave up my career for you. [*Laughter*]

PLAYBOY: Do you see ordinary people almost resenting your attitude? Saying you understand what a housewife feels, John, yet you're just doing it as a lark?

LENNON: No, it wasn't a lark. The serious intent was

to orchestrate what went into the baby's mind and body on a full-time basis for at least five years. And it's not over now just 'cause we're making this album. In fact, I'm worried that Sean is away from my influence too much now. Like, he's put on a couple of pounds because I'm not watching his diet, and as soon as this album's tucked away I'll go back and reestablish my position with him because I need it and he needs it. You know, the Catholic Church used to say, "Give me the child for five or seven years and I will give you the man." I wanted to be there for that. That's the main concern I have—that I made the right moves. I've been very, very careful. There's been no lightheartedness about that.

ONO: And he did it well.

PLAYBOY: But what about the maternal role itself? Did you ever come out with, "Goddamn it, Yoko, you *are* the mother!"?

LENNON: I probably did. [*To Yoko*] Did I say that?

ONO: Well, initially you said it didn't matter, anybody can be the mother. But then you started to realize that the child missed his *mother,* that there *is* a connection. And I started to realize it, too. The blood connection. Which is very strange.

PLAYBOY: Yoko, you say you started to realize it, but you have said you weren't really much of a mother when it came to day-to-day?

ONO: I don't know what it is. I think it probably had something to do with the fact that I was brought up by nannies. It's almost like the attitude a mother has with a sick child: She'd like to take care of him herself, but she has the doctors take care of him instead. I don't know.

LENNON: She likes to come on with "Maybe I don't have a mother instinct; I was brought up by a nanny." She gets macho because she's been playing this macho game for five or six years.

ONO: Many different facets.

LENNON: You have many facets, but you're not a bad mother, so don't try to sell yourself as one.

ONO: I know I'm not a bad mother. . . .

PLAYBOY: Is Sean aware you were a Beatle? To what extent have you protected Sean from your Beatle fame, your Beatle past?

LENNON: Beatles was never mentioned to him. There was no reason to. We never played Beatles records— unlike the story that went around that I was sittin' in the kitchen for five years playin' Beatles records like some kind of Howard Hughes. Once he was over at a friend's and *Yellow Submarine* was on television, and he came running over saying, "Daddy, were you a Beatle?"

PLAYBOY: He had no concept of the Beatles before that?

LENNON: He didn't differentiate between the Beatles and daddy and mummy. He thinks Yoko is a Beatle, too. He knows that there's a Ringo and a Paul and a George and these people that somehow used to be around. But children can't conceive of what goes on before they're born.

PLAYBOY: But now, does he think of the Beatles the same way he might think of some musical group he knows?

LENNON: No, because he hasn't been exposed to them. I think I let him have one Beatles record when he expressed an interest, once he got this idea that there was some singing going on. But I generally keep them away from him. I don't have any Beatles records on our jukebox. He's more exposed to early rock 'n' roll—Chuck Berry and Elvis. He's into "Hound Dog" now because he thinks it's about hunting! [*Laughter*]

PLAYBOY: Why don't you want him exposed to Beatles music?

LENNON: Because I can't stand hearing them all the time! Because I have to relive the sessions. It's not because I hate Beatle music. It's like reading an old diary all the time. There's a time to go through your old snapshots, but most of the time you're too busy livin' now. So I don't hate the music. If it comes on the radio, it's a different matter.

PLAYBOY: One more Beatles-related topic. So far you've talked a lot about John and Yoko and Paul and Ringo—but you haven't said much about George. Why?

LENNON: I'll tell you why it is. George put a book out [*I, Me, Mine*] privately and I was hurt by it, so this message will go out to him. By glaring omission in the book, my influence on his life is absolutely zilch and nil. Not mentioned. In his book, which is purportedly this clarity of vision of each song he wrote and its influences, he remembers every two-bit sax player or guitarist he met in subsequent years. I'm not in the book.

PLAYBOY: Why?

LENNON: Because George's relationship with me was one of young follower and older guy. He's three or four years younger than me. It's a love-hate relationship, and I think George still bears resentment toward me for being a daddy who left home. He would not agree with this, but that's my feeling about it. I was just hurt. I was just left out, as if I didn't exist.

I don't want to be that egomaniacal, but he was like a disciple of mine when we started. I was already an art student when Paul and George were still in grammar school [high school in the United States]. There is a vast difference between being in high school and being in college, and I was already in college and already had sexual relationships, already drank and did a lot of things like that.

When George was a kid, he used to follow me and my first girl friend, Cynthia—who became my wife—around. Cynthia and I would come out of the art school together and he'd be hovering around like those kids at the gate of the Dakota now. He was literally like that! Cyn and I would be going to a coffee shop or a movie and George would follow us down the street two hundred yards behind. And Cyn would say, as Yoko will say now, "Who *is* that guy? What's he want?" I'd say,

"He just wants to hang out. Should we take him with us?" She'd say, "Oh, OK, let's take him to the bloody movies." So we'd allow him to come to the movies with us. And that's the sort of relationship it was. He turned a little nasty later on. Maybe he saw I wasn't the man he envisioned.

ONO: Well, I tell you truthfully, I don't think he really meant it. The book was probably edited by people around him. I know some people around him who have a lot of influence on him.

LENNON: I don't agree. I don't agree. You haven't read the book.

ONO: Yeah, but I think—

LENNON: Well then, read the book before you talk. In the book there's a comment after each song he wrote.

ONO: Yes, but I think he was strongly advised not to mention—

LENNON: Not mentioned once! I remember the day he called to ask for help on "Taxman," one of his first songs. I threw in a few one-liners to help the song along, because that's what he asked for. He came to me because he couldn't go to Paul, because Paul wouldn't have helped him at that period. I didn't want to do it. I thought, Oh, no, don't tell me I have to work on George's stuff. It's enough doing my own and Paul's. But because I loved him and I didn't want to hurt him when he called that afternoon and said, "Will you help me with this song?" I just sort of bit my tongue and said OK. It had been John and Paul so long, he'd been left out because he hadn't been a songwriter up until then. As a singer, we allowed him only one track on each album. If you listen to the Beatles' first albums, the English versions, he gets a single track. The songs he and Ringo sang at first were the songs that used to be part of my repertoire in the dance halls. I used to pick the easier songs for them to sing. So I am slightly resentful of George's book.

PLAYBOY: How did you feel about the lawsuit George

lost that claimed the music to "My Sweet Lord" is a rip-off of the Chiffons' hit "He's So Fine"?*

LENNON: Well, he walked right into it. He knew what he was doing.

PLAYBOY: Are you saying he consciously plagiarized the song?

LENNON: He must have known, you know. He's smarter than that. It's irrelevant, actually—only on a monetary level does it matter. In the early years, I'd often carry around someone else's song in my head, and only when I'd put it down on tape—because I can't write music—would I consciously change it to my own melody because I knew that otherwise somebody would sue me. George could have changed a few bars in that song and nobody could have ever touched him, but he just let it go and paid the price. Maybe he thought God would just sort of let him off.

PLAYBOY: Are—

LENNON: I'd like to clarify that. You see, I am slightly resentful of George's book, but don't get me wrong—I still love those guys. The Beatles are over, but John, Paul, George, and Ringo go on. I mean, just because I'm upset about George's book doesn't mean that's all I feel. Do you understand? I like them and it's over. Get it? [*Laughing*] I don't want to start another whole thing between me and George just because of the way I feel today. Tomorrow I will feel absolutely differently. It's not important, anyway. I don't feel that or anything *only* about him or any of them. It's very complicated and there are a lot of mixed emotions about all of them. That's why it's difficult to say *anything*. I don't want to come off niggling. It's stupid inasmuch as the repercussions are not worth some sort of offhand remarks about each other.

---

*The courts found George Harrison guilty of "subconscious" plagiarism and ordered him to pay $587,000.

23

*Barry was off to his office, and Yoko to a meeting,
leaving me in John's care. We began, as he called it,
the Beatles' memory lane trip—which turned into much
more.*

*To start, he asked Fred, working in the outer office,
to gather up his collection of records to use as a
reference. A songbook had a chronological list of Beatles
songs. I spread the books and records on the floor of
Yoko's office and John and I took our places lounging
on the carpet.*

LENNON: OK, if you want to pursue a certain song in
depth, you ask me; otherwise, I'll just give you the
surface memory that comes to me.

PLAYBOY: Right. Let's go more or less chronologi-
cally. Starting with "Love Me Do."

LENNON: "Love Me Do" is Paul's song. He wrote it
when he was a teen-ager. Let me think . . . [*sings*]
"Love, love me *do*. . . ." I might have helped on the
middle eight, but I couldn't swear to it. I do know he
had the song around, in Hamburg even, way, way
before we were songwriters.

PLAYBOY: With these early love songs, were they
about your girl friends, your love life?

LENNON: They were basically made up. They weren't
about real situations. I think "In My Life" was the first
song that I wrote that was really, consciously about my
life, and it was sparked by a remark a journalist and
writer in England made after *In His Own Write* came
out. I *think* "In My Life" was after *In His Own
Write*. . . . But he said to me, "Why don't you put

some of the way you write in the book, as it were, in the songs? Or why don't you put something about your childhood into the songs?'' Which came out later as ''Penny Lane'' from Paul—although it was actually me who lived in Penny Lane—and ''Strawberry Fields.''

PLAYBOY: It never dawned on you before to write from your own experience?

LENNON: Yeah, we were just writing songs a la Everly Brothers, a la Buddy Holly, pop songs with no more thought to them than that—to create a sound. And the words were almost irrelevant.

PLAYBOY: Go on.

LENNON: ''In My Life'' started out as a bus journey from my house on 250 Menlove Avenue to town, mentioning every place that I could remember. And it was ridiculous. This is before even ''Penny Lane'' was written and I had Penny Lane, Strawberry Fields, Tram Sheds—Tram Sheds are the depot just outside of Penny Lane—and it was the most boring sort of ''What I Did on My Holidays Bus Trip'' song and it wasn't working at all. I can*not* do this! I cannot do this!

But then I laid back and these lyrics started coming to me about the places I remember. Now Paul helped write the middle-eight melody. The whole lyrics were already written before Paul had even heard it. In ''In My Life,'' his contribution melodically was the harmony and the middle eight itself.

PLAYBOY: Penny Lane is a street?

LENNON: Penny Lane is not only a street but it's a district. It's like Times Square or Columbus Avenue. When you say Columbus Avenue, you mean the whole area. Penny Lane is a suburban district where, until age four, I lived with my mother and father, although my father was a sailor, always at sea, and my grandfather. In one of those row houses like they always picture the early Beatles' life in *Yellow Submarine* and other, you know, dreamy versions of the poor, working-class lads. But after that I lived in Penny Lane on a street called

Newcastle Road. So I was the only Beatle that lived in Penny Lane.

PLAYBOY: And "Strawberry Fields Forever"?

LENNON: "Strawberry Fields" I wrote when I was making "How I Won the War" in Almería, Spain.

PLAYBOY: Was that right after you met Yoko?

LENNON: No.

PLAYBOY: You said earlier that you had met Yoko and that's when you knew you were starting to drift from the Beatles.

LENNON: No, no. I was starting to drift from the Beatles before Yoko. What I did . . . in my own cowardly way was *use* Yoko . . . it was like now I have the strength to leave because I know there is another side to life.

But in the period 1966 after the Beatles stopped touring—which was the last tour, the Jesus Christ Tour, I call it. Right? When the Klan and all those people were howling at me for an offhand remark, right?

PLAYBOY: That "the Beatles were bigger than Christ"?

LENNON: Yeah. Then Dick Lester offered me the part in this movie, which gave me time to think without going home. We were in Almería, and it took me six weeks to write the song. I was writing it all the time I was making the film. And as anybody knows about film work, there's a lot of hanging around.

I have an original tape of it somewhere. Of how it sounded before it became the sort of psychedelic-sounding song it became on record. I probably have "In My Life," too. I have the tapes of "We Can Work It Out" somewhere with Paul singing it, double-track guitar on a home tape.

PLAYBOY: How long after that did you meet Yoko?

LENNON: My memory is great for details and everything, but dates I'm not good at.

PLAYBOY: Just as far as the chronology goes . . .

LENNON: I came back from Spain and the movie. It's just sort of a blank period because it was the end of the tour and I came back from Spain and Brian died then.

The Maharishi appeared, Brian died, Yoko appeared. I mean, so much went on at that period that I can't get the sequence right, you know? It must all have been around the same period. So if you found out when the film was made . . . I could tell you what happened. . . . It seems impossible that everything happened in 1966!

PLAYBOY: Let's go on with "Strawberry Fields." It was a place, right?

LENNON: Yeah, I took the name as an image. You know, it's like *A Little Night Music* was from that Magritte painting of a black tree with half a silver moon on it. It's irrelevant to the musical, except to know that the guy saw that picture and got this idea or whatever.

After I left Penny Lane, I moved in with my auntie, who lived in the suburbs in a nice semidetached place with a small garden and doctors and lawyers and that ilk living around, not the poor, slummy kind of image that was projected. I was a nice clean-cut suburban boy, and in the class system that was about a half a niche higher-class than Paul, George, and Ringo, who lived in government-subsidized houses. We owned our own house, had our own garden, and they didn't have anything like that. So I was a bit of a fruit compared to them, in a way. You know, I was a suburban kid and they were all—well, Ringo was the only real city kid. Anyway, we're digressing now. What was the question?

PLAYBOY: "Strawberry Fields" is . . .

LENNON: It's a Salvation Army home that was near the house I lived in with my auntie in the suburbs. There were two famous houses there. One was owned by Gladstone, which was a reformatory for boys, which I could see out my window. And Strawberry Fields was just around the corner from that. It was an old Victorian house converted for Salvation Army orphans, and as a kid I used to go to their garden parties with my friends Ivan, Nigel, and Pete. We'd all go up there and hang out and sell lemonade bottles for a penny and we always had fun at Strawberry Fields. Apparently, it used to be a farm that made strawberries or whatever. I don't know. But I just took the name—it had nothing to do with the Salvation Army. As an image—Strawberry Fields forever.

PLAYBOY: What about the lyrics: "Living is easy ..."?

LENNON: ". . . with eyes closed, misunderstanding all you see." It still goes now, doesn't it? Aren't I saying exactly the same thing now?

PLAYBOY: Was that idea a new awakening for you?

LENNON: No, it wasn't a new awakening. It was the fact that I was putting it on paper. I was awake all my life. You understand? I've always been, all my life.

PLAYBOY: Well before the Beatles?

LENNON: You can't isolate things like that. It's like . . . the constant search for why you go down one road and why you go down another. It has as much to do with being from Liverpool or being from Quarry Bank Grammar School or being in a household where the library was full of Oscar Wilde and Whistler and Fitzgerald and all the Book of the Month Club stuff that my auntie had around, and her taking in students when my uncle died and, therefore, being exposed to eighteen-year-old intelligent minds who were becoming vets and chemists and all, and me being a young boy surrounded by this. . . . Which influence is more? It's you and your ilk—I use that in a friendly way—the Beatle watchers—who are so hung up on Beatles. It always comes off like I'm attacking the Beatles. I'm saying that the Beatles were important, but in my life the Beatles influence . . . was it more important than my birth, my education? The fact that my parents split and I lived with my auntie? I cannot give that more important emphasis than any other part of my life. So the awareness that is apparently trying to be expressed in "Strawberry Fields" . . .

Let's say, in one way, I was always "hip," man. I was hip in kindergarten. I was different from others *then*. I was different all my life. It's not a case of, Then he took acid and woke up, or Then he had a marijuana joint and woke up. It's not that at all. Everything is as important as everything else.

My influences are tremendous, from Lewis Carroll to Oscar Wilde to tough little kids that used to live near me who ended up in prison and things like that. And the Beatles were only ten years! I've lived with Yoko longer than I was a Beatle! But people don't understand that. I've been with Yoko longer than I was with Paul, OK? But still they ask about Paul. Obviously the most important influence in my life for the last thirteen years has been Yoko Ono, and there's no getting away from that. Now, I've got another forty or fifty years to live, or maybe longer, whatever it is. And who knows, so what the hell.

"Strawberry Fields" is my attempt at expressing that. The second line goes, "No one I think is in my tree." Well, what I was trying to say in that line is "Nobody seems to be as hip as me, therefore I must be crazy or a genius." It's that same problem I had when I was five: "There is something wrong with me because I seem to see things other people don't see. Am I crazy, or am I a genius?" I don't think I'm either: crazy and genius don't really *mean* anything anymore. I don't literally mean genius as the things we deify, but as the spirit of genius that can come through anybody at any given time. And if there is such a thing, well, I'm going to *be* one. It was like, "If there is a leader of the Beatles, I'm it." If there ain't, then it's a democracy. It sort of covers all angles.

So the line says, "No one I think is in my tree, I mean it must be high or low." What I'm saying, in my insecure way, is "Nobody seems to understand where I'm coming from. I seem to see things in a different way from most people." I mean, I would see teachers and fully sense the underlying stupidity or surfaceness of the situation. So at thirteen, fourteen, I would think, *Yes,* this guy is an asshole and I am seeing his subconscious; I can read his mind; I'm picking up things that he doesn't even know exist. Meaning I always was so psychic or intuitive and poetic, or whatever you want to call it, that I was always seeing things in a hallucinatory way that always saw beyond the mask. And it's scary when you're a child, because there is nobody to relate to. Neither my auntie nor my friends nor anybody could *ever* see it! And it's very, very scary. The only contact I had was reading something about Oscar Wilde or Dylan Thomas or Vincent Van Gogh — of the suffering they went through because of their vision. They were *seeing* and being tortured by society for trying to express what they were . . . that loneliness and seeing what *is*. . . .

It isn't egomania. It's a fact. If somebody gave me a pair of glasses that makes me see through walls, I can't help it. It doesn't make me better or worse than anybody else; I just see and hear *differently* from other people—the same way musicians hear music differently from nonmusicians. And there is no way of explaining it, there is no . . .

PLAYBOY: You never found people who shared your visions?

LENNON: Only dead people in books. Lewis Carroll, certain paintings I would see. Surrealism had a great effect on me because then I realized that the imagery in my mind wasn't insanity—that if it was insane, then I belonged to an exclusive club that sees the world in those terms. Surrealism to me is reality. Psychedelic vision is reality to me and always was. When I looked at myself in the mirror at twelve, thirteen—when you become very conscious as a teen-ager of your appearance, and spend a lot of time combing your hair—I used to, literally, trance out into alpha. I didn't know what it was called then. I only found out years later that there is a name for those conditions. But I would find myself seeing these hallucinatory images of my face changing, becoming cosmic and complete. I would start trancing out and the eyes would get bigger and the room would vanish; I read the same description years later by a famous person who took opium.

PLAYBOY: You started to say that was only one part of you.

LENNON: Yeah. [*Dreamy-eyed and reflective*] I always was a rebel because of whatever sociological thing gave me a chip on the shoulder. But on the other hand, I want to be loved and accepted. That's why I'm on stage, like a performing flea. It's because I would like to belong. A part of me would like to be accepted by all facets of society and *not* be this loudmouth, lunatic, poet/musician. But I cannot be what I'm not. What the hell do you do? You want to belong but you don't want to belong because you cannot belong.

It's like, well, at school again. You know, at grammar school when they ask you, "What do you want to be?" I would say, "Well, a journalist." I never would dare to say, "An artist," because in the social background that I came from, I used to say to my auntie, "You read about artists and you worship them in museums, but you don't want them living around the house." All right? So the teachers said, "No, something real." And I'd say, "Well, present me with some alternative." They'd suggest veterinarian, doctor, dentist, lawyer. And I knew there was no hope in *hell* of me ever becoming that. So there was never anywhere for me to go.

PLAYBOY: But even then you were optimistic, positive: in "Strawberry Fields" you say, "Somehow it all works out."

LENNON: Yeah. I mean, it's like a little gag that the Beatles used. When the Beatles were depressed, we had this thing that I would chant and they would answer. It was from a cheap movie they made about Liverpool years ago. And in it they say, "Where are we going, Johnny?" or something, and the leader of the gang would say, "We're going to burn this" or "We're going to stomp on that." Well, I would say to the others when we were all depressed, thinking that the group was going nowhere, this is a shitty deal, we're in a shitty dressing room—I would say, "Where are we going, fellows?'' And they would go, ''To the top, Johnny'' in pseudo-American voices. And I would say, ''Where is that, fellows?'' And they would say, ''To the toppermost of the poppermost.'' I would say, ''Right!'' And we would all cheer up.

PLAYBOY: So with the downs, and the scary mysticism, you still were optimistic.

LENNON: Yeah. The other expression I had which became a Beatle expression, but was actually mine, was ''It will turn up all right in the end.'' I used to say that to my friend Pete who was in the Quarrymen, which is the name of the group before it turned into the Beatles—before Paul was in it. Pete would worry about exams at grammar school. The original group was named after my school, which was Quarry Bank, and had a Latin motto which meant ''out of this rock''—that's symbolic, isn't it?—''you will find truth.''

Anyway, we always failed the exams and never did any work and Pete was always worried about his future. I would say that—''don't worry, it'll work out''—to him and the gang that was around me then—because I always had a gang; I was always the leader of a little gang of guys, you know. The usual trip; the Beatles became my new gang. I always had a group of three or four or five guys around with me who would play various roles in my life, supportive and, you know, subservient. In general, me being the bullyboy.

But I always believed that something would turn up. I didn't make plans for the future. I didn't study for the exam. I didn't put a little bit on the side. I wasn't *capable* of doing it. Therefore, I was the one that all the other boys' parents—including Paul's father—would say, ''Keep away from him.'' Because they knew what I was. The parents instinctively recognized I was a troublemaker, meaning I did not conform and I would influence their children, which I did. I did my best to disrupt every friend's home there was. Partly out of envy that I didn't have this so-called home . . . but I *did*. I *had* an auntie and an uncle and a nice suburban home, thank you very much. This image of me being the orphan is garbage because I was well protected by my auntie and my uncle and they looked after me very well, thanks. So . . . and that's for her, my auntie, because she objects to a remark Paul made saying that I probably was spending all this time with Sean now because I never had a family life—it's absolute rubbish.

There were five women that were my family. Five *strong, intelligent, beautiful* women, five sisters. One happened to be my mother. My mother just couldn't deal with life. She was the youngest. And she had a husband who ran away to sea and the war was on and she couldn't cope with me and I ended up living with her elder sister.

Now those women were fantastic. One day I might do a kind of *Forsyte Saga* just about them. I always had it in the back of my mind, because they were fantastic women and they dominated the situation in all the family. The men were just invisible in our family. I was always with the women. I always heard them talk about the men and talk about life, and they always knew what was going on. The men never, never ever knew.

And that was my first feminist education. And with that knowledge and the fact that I wasn't tied to *parents*— that was the difference—I would infiltrate the other boys' minds. I could say, "Parents are not gods because I don't live with mine and, therefore, I know." I could say to Paul "If you want to wear tight pants, Paul, tell your father to screw himself." His father knew I would say that to him. And it went for all my friends. . . . That was the gift I got of not having parents. I cried a lot about not having them, but I also had the gift of awareness of *not* being something. . . .
PLAYBOY: You learned that all at an early age.
LENNON: Right. Most people never got out of it. Some people cannot see that their parents are still torturing them, even when they are in their forties and fifties— they still have that strangle-hold over them and their thoughts and their minds. I never had that fear of and

adulation for parents. Well, that's the gift of being a so-called orphan—which I never was at all. [*John was now filled with emotion, the words tumbling out in free association.*] My mother was alive and lived a fifteen-minute walk away from me all my life. I saw her sporadically off and on all the time. I just didn't live with her.

PLAYBOY: She's not alive, is she?

LENNON: No, she got killed by an off-duty cop who was drunk. She was just at the bus stop and he ran her down in a car. So that was another big trauma for me. I lost her twice. Once as a five-year-old when I was moved in with my auntie. And once again at fifteen when she actually, physically died. And that was *very* traumatic for me. I was at art school. So I must have been sixteen. So it must have been 1956. And that was . . . really a hard time for me. It just absolutely made me *very*, very bitter. The underlying chip on my shoulder that I had as a youth got *really* big then. Being a teen-ager and a rock 'n' roller *and* an art student *and* my mother being killed just when I was reestablishing a relationship with her . . .

PLAYBOY: What about—

LENNON: . . . it was *very* traumatic for me.

PLAYBOY: —what about your dad?

LENNON: Whereas Paul had lost his mother but he never lost his father.

PLAYBOY: Yes, he lost his mother very young. At about three.

LENNON: Yeah . . . well, my father had gone away to sea and I never saw him again until I made a lot of money and he came back. Which is another story altogether.

PLAYBOY: What happened?

LENNON: I opened the *Daily Express* and there he was, washing dishes in a small hotel or something very near to where I was living in the Stockbroker Belt outside of London. And he was blackmailing me. . . . The story he told the media was that he had been writing to me to try and get in contact but I didn't want to see him. I was too upset about it all. He *would* turn up when I was rich and famous and not bother to turn up before. . . . So I wasn't going to see him at all, but he sort of blackmailed me in the press and I fell for it and saw him and we had some kind of relationship and then he died a few years later of cancer. But at sixty-five he married a twenty-two-year-old secretary that had been working for me or the Beatles, and had a child, which I thought was hopeful for a man who had lived a life of a drunk and almost a Bowery bum. A lot of his life was spent like that.

PLAYBOY: Sounds like a scene from a melodrama.

LENNON: Well, everybody—like Yoko was saying before—if you go into anybody's life, there's *amazing* things that went on. It just seems so dramatic when it's somebody so-called famous. That's why I like autobiographies. It is the little decisions that are made, those sort of decisions which change the whole person's direction. And who knows whether they make the decision or it's made for them or what? So I don't regret any of it, the suffering or the happiness.

My childhood was not all suffering. It was not all slum. I was always *well* dressed, *well* fed, *well* schooled, and brought up to be a nice lower-middle-class English boy. You know? And that's what made the Beatles different, the fact that George, Paul, and John were *grammar* school boys. Up till then, all rock-and-rollers basically had been black and poor, rural South or whatever, city slums. And the whites had been truckers like Elvis. Buddy Holly was apparently more of our ilk, a bit of a suburban boy who had learned to read and write and knew a little more. But the so-called thing of the Beatles was the fact that we were pretty well educated and not truckers. Paul could have gone to university. He was *always* a good boy. He passed his exams. He could have become, what the hell—I don't know—Dr. McCartney, I suppose. I could have done it meself if I had worked. I never worked.

PLAYBOY: Dr. Lennon?
LENNON: Well, I could have taken up fine arts or languages—that kind of stuff. The arts I know I could have handled easily. It just was never encouraged. They only wanted scientists in the Fifties. And artsy-fartsy people were just spies. They still *are* in society.
PLAYBOY: Is your aunt still living?
LENNON: She is living in Pool Dorset in a house by herself because that's what she chooses to do.
PLAYBOY: How about your uncle?
LENNON: No, he died right around the same period as my mother, within a few years of each other.

24

John was winding down as Yoko returned to her office. After a cup of tea, John volunteered to vacate the office so Yoko could carry on her business. We packed up the pile of records and books and set up in the outer office. There, however, the noise was intolerable—phones, people rushing in and out, music in the background. John shrugged. "Let's try it in here."

I followed him. John plopped down on the cold marble floor of a huge bathroom. "How's this?" he asked. I closed the door, and there we sat for hours. Our voices echoed loudly in the naked room's whiteness.

PLAYBOY: I'll never hear "Strawberry Fields" the same again. Okay. More songs. "Do You Want to Know a Secret?" Isn't that one you wrote for George?
LENNON: Well, I can't say I wrote it *for* George. I was in the first apartment I'd ever had that wasn't shared by fourteen other students—gals and guys at art school. I'd just married Cyn, and Brian Epstein gave

us his secret little apartment that he kept in Liverpool
for his sexual liaisons separate from his home life. And
he let Cyn and I have that apartment.

My mother was always . . . she was a comedienne
and a singer. Not professional, but, you know, she used
to get up in pubs and things like that. She had a good
voice. She could do Kay Starr. She used to do this little
tune when I was just a one- or two-year-old . . . yeah,
she was still living with me then. . . . The tune was
from the Disney movie—[*singing*] "Want to know a
secret? Promise not to tell. You are standing by a
wishing well."

So, I had this sort of thing in my head and I wrote it
and just gave it to George to sing. I thought it would be
a good vehicle for him because it only had three notes
and he wasn't the best singer in the world. He has
improved a lot since then, but in those days his singing
ability was very poor because (a) he hadn't had the
opportunity, and (b) he concentrated more on the guitar.
So I wrote that—not for *him* as I was writing it, but
when I *had* written it, I thought he could do it. It was
just written.

Like "I'm Happy Just to Dance with You" in "Hard
Day's Night"—that was written *for* George to give him
a piece of the action. That's another reason why I was
hurt a bit by his book, because I even went to the
trouble of making sure he got the "B" side of a Beatles
single, because he hadn't even gotten a "B" side until
. . . "Something" was the first time he ever got an
"A" side because Paul and I always either wrote both
sides anyway. . . . Not because we were keeping him
out; 'cause, simply, his material wasn't up to scratch.
That's the reality of it. It wasn't a conspiracy. He just
didn't have the material.

PLAYBOY: Was it the same as when Ringo—
LENNON: But I made sure George got the "B" side
of "The Ballad of John and Yoko," I think. And those
little things he doesn't remember. You know, I always
tried . . . it was because of me that Ringo and George

got a piece of John and Paul's songwriting. Under Allen Klein's auspices, John and Paul own completely anything that Maclen published, and I always felt bad that George and Ringo didn't get a piece of the publishing. Not bad enough to do anything about it, but slightly guilty about it. And under Klein's maneuvering-and-management period, when the opportunity came to give them only five percent each of Maclen—which is still a lot of money for songwriting—it was because of me that they got it. Not because of Klein and not because of Paul, because of me. Paul had to say "yes" because he couldn't say no. But it was under my instigation that they got it.

Now, *I* don't get a piece of George's songs. I don't get a piece of anything he wrote, like "Something," or any of Ringo's songs. Not even . . . anything. Okay? Or the contributions I made to George's early songs like "Taxman." Never asked for anything or any recognition or anything from it. And that's why I might have sounded resentful about George and Ringo, because of the Apple business going on and the attitude they conveyed that somehow "John has forsaken us and John is tricking us." It just wasn't true.

PLAYBOY: Isn't some of the trouble due to the fact that you and Paul are seen as the songwriting Beatles?

LENNON: Let's say, I think it's possible for John and Paul to have created the same thing with two other guys. It may *not* have been possible for George and Ringo to have created it without John and Paul. OK?

PLAYBOY: And the fact that they know that—

LENNON: But that doesn't take away from the individual talents that they have. Ringo was a star in his own right in Liverpool before we even met. Ringo was a professional drummer who sang and performed and was in one of the top groups in Britain, but especially in Liverpool. So Ringo's talent would have come out one way or the other. I don't know what he would have ended up as—whatever that spark is in Ringo, we all know it but we can't put our finger on it. Whether it's acting, drumming, or singing, I don't know. There's something in him that is projectable and he would have surfaced as an individual.

PLAYBOY: But getting back to the point you made about how the Beatles could have been you and Paul and two other guys—wouldn't *that* be the reason for Ringo and George's resentment?

LENNON: It probably could have worked like that. But maybe, on the other hand, who knows? It mightn't have worked without them. So there is no way . . . it is all. What was your fate before you were born? It is speculation.

PLAYBOY: What about Ringo's drumming?

LENNON: Ringo's a damn good drummer. He was always a good drummer. He's not *technically* good, but I think Ringo's drumming is underrated the same way as Paul's bass playing is underrated.

Paul was one of the most innovative bass players that ever played bass, and half the stuff that's going on now is directly ripped off from his Beatles period. He was coy about his bass playing. He's an egomaniac about everything else, but his bass playing he was always a bit coy about. He is a great musician who plays the bass like few other people could play it. If you compare his bass playing with the Rolling Stones' bass playing and you compare Ringo's drumming with Charlie Watts's drumming, they are equal to them, if not better. I always objected to the fact that because Charlie came on a little more "arty" than Ringo, and knew jazz and did cartoons, that he got credit. I think that Charlie's a damn good drummer and the other's a good bass player. But I think Paul and Ringo stand up anywhere with *any* of the rock musicians. Not technically great. None of us were technical musicians. None of us could read music. None of us can write it. But as pure musicians, as inspired humans to make noise, they're as good as anybody!

PLAYBOY: All right. "P.S. I Love You."

LENNON: That's Paul's song. He was trying to write

a "Soldier Boy" like the Shirelles. He wrote that in Germany or when we were going to and from Hamburg. I might have contributed something. I can't remember anything in particular. It was mainly his song.

PLAYBOY: "Please Please Me."

LENNON: "Please Please Me" is my song completely. It was my attempt at writing a Roy Orbison song, would you believe it? I wrote it in the bedroom in my house at Menlove Avenue, which was my auntie's place. . . . I remember the day and the pink eyelet on the bed and I heard Roy Orbison doing "Only the Lonely" or something. That's where that came from. And also I was always intrigued by the words of [*sings*] "Please, lend your little ears to my pleas"—a Bing Crosby song. I was always intrigued by the double use of the word "please." So it was a combination of Bing Crosby and Roy Orbison.

PLAYBOY: "From Me to You," you said, was the one you and Paul did in a van.

LENNON: Yeah. We were writing it in a car, I think, and I think the first line was mine. I mean, I know it was mine. [*Hums melody of first line.*] And then after that we took it from there. It was far bluesier than that when we wrote it. The notes—today you could rearrange it pretty funky. We were just writing the next single after "She Loves You."

PLAYBOY: What *about* "She Loves You"?

LENNON: It was written together and I don't know how. I remember it was Paul's idea: Instead of singing "I love you" again, we'd have a third party. That kind of little detail is apparently in his work now where he will write a story about someone and I'm more inclined to just write about myself.

PLAYBOY: Was that the first one that had the "yeahs" in it?

LENNON: Yeah-yeah-yeah. Yeah.

PLAYBOY: Where did that stuff come from?

LENNON: The "woo woo" was taken from the Isley Brothers' "Twist and Shout," which we stuck into everything—"From Me to You," "She Loves You," they had all that "woo woo."

PLAYBOY: And the "yeah-yeah-yeah"?

LENNON: The "yeah-yeah" I don't know.

PLAYBOY: It became identified with you.

LENNON: Yeah, but there have been *lots* of "oh yeah" and "yeah" and "uh-huh" in rock 'n' roll. Lonnie Donegan always did it. He was a Britisher who had done a lot of American folk music. And I remember Elvis did that in "All Shook Up." But I can't remember how we got the "yeah-yeah-yeah" for sure.

PLAYBOY: "Thank You Girl."

LENNON: "Thank You Girl" was one of our efforts at writing a single that didn't work. So it became a "B" side or an album track.

PLAYBOY: "Misery."

LENNON: "Misery"—[*singing*] "The world is feeling bad, misery." It was kind of a John song more than a Paul song, but it was written together.

PLAYBOY: "I Call Your Name."

LENNON: That was my song. When there was no Beatles and no group. I just had it around. It was my effort as a kind of blues originally, and then I wrote the middle eight just to stick it in the album when it came out years later. The first part had been written before Hamburg even. It was one of my *first* attempts at a song.

PLAYBOY: "I'll Be on My Way."

LENNON: That's Paul, through and through. Doesn't it sound like him? Tra la la la la [*laughs*]. Yeah, that's Paul on the voids of driving through the country.

PLAYBOY: "Bad to Me."

LENNON: "Bad to Me" I wrote for Billy J. Kramer. Specifically for Billy J. Kramer. I was on holiday with Brian Epstein in Spain, where the rumors went around that he and I were having a love affair. Well, it was almost a love affair, but not quite. It was never consummated. But it was a pretty intense relationship.

It was my first experience with a homosexual that I

was conscious *was* homosexual. He had admitted it to me. We had this holiday together because Cyn was pregnant, and I went to Spain and there were lots of funny stories. We used to sit in a café in Torremolinos looking at all the boys and I'd say, "Do you like that one, do you like this one?" I was rather enjoying the experience, thinking like a writer all the time: *I am experiencing this*, you know. And while he was out on the tiles one night, or lying asleep with a hangover one afternoon, I remember playing him the song "Bad to Me." That was a commissioned song, done for Billy J. Kramer, who was another of Brian's singers. From Liverpool.

PLAYBOY: "It Won't Be Long."

LENNON: "It Won't Be Long" is mine. It was my attempt at writing another single. It never quite made it. That was the one where the guy in the *London Times* wrote about the "Aeolian cadences of the chords"— which started the whole intellectual bit about Beatles.

PLAYBOY: "All My Loving."

LENNON: "All My Loving" is Paul, I regret to say. Ha-ha-ha.

PLAYBOY: Why?

LENNON: Because it's a damn good piece of work. [*Singing*] "All my loving . . ." But I play a pretty mean guitar in back.

PLAYBOY: "Little Child."

LENNON: "Little Child" was another effort of Paul and I to write a song for somebody. It was probably Ringo.

PLAYBOY: "Hold Me Tight."

LENNON: That was Paul's. Maybe I stuck some bits in there—I don't remember. It was a pretty poor song and I was never really interested in it either way.

PLAYBOY: How about "I Wanna Be Your Man"?

LENNON: "I Wanna Be Your Man" was a kind of lick Paul had: "I want to be your lover, baby. I want to be your man." I think we finished it off for the Stones . . . yeah, we were taken down to meet the Stones at

the club where they were playing in Richmond by Brian
and some other guy. They wanted a song and we went
to see them to see what kind of stuff they did. Mick and
Keith had heard that we had an unfinished song—Paul
just had this bit and we needed another verse or something. We sort of played it roughly to them and they
said, "Yeah, OK, that's our style." So Paul and I just
went off in the corner of the room and finished the song
off while they were all still there talking. We came back
and that's how Mick and Keith got inspired to write,
because, "Jesus, look at that. They just went in the
corner and wrote it and came back!" Right in front of
their eyes we did it.

So we gave it to them. It was a throwaway. The only
two versions of the song were Ringo and the Rolling
Stones. That shows how much importance we put on it:
We weren't going to give them anything *great*, right? I
believe it was the Stones' first record.

PLAYBOY: "I'll Keep You Satisfied."

LENNON: Paul's.

PLAYBOY: "Love of the Loved."

LENNON: That's another one of Paul's written when
he was a teen-ager and sort of resurrected later on in the
Beatle years.

PLAYBOY: "I'm in Love."

LENNON: That sounds like me. I don't remember a
hell of a thing about it.

PLAYBOY: "Hello Little Girl."

LENNON: That was me. That was actually my first
song. [*Singing*] "When I see you every day I say mmm
hmm, hello little girl." I remembered some Thirties or
Forties song which was [*singing*] "You're delightful,
you're delicious and da da da. Isn't it a pity that you are
such a scatterbrain." [*Laughing*] That always fascinated
me for some reason or another. It's also connected to
me mother. It's all very Freudian. She used to sing that
one. So I made "Hello Little Girl" out of it.

PLAYBOY: "Can't Buy Me Love."

LENNON: That's Paul's completely. Maybe I had something to do with the chorus, but I don't know. I always considered it his song.

PLAYBOY: "From a Window."

LENNON: That's Paul's. That's his artsy period with Jane Asher. I'm not sure.

PLAYBOY: "Like Dreamers Do."

LENNON: That's Paul. That was another one that he'd written as a teen-ager and sort of resurrected and polished up for later on. That's on the audition tape that we sent Decca which is around as a bootleg. I sing "To Know Her Is to Love Her" and "Hello Little Girl" and Paul sings "Like Dreamers Do." I believe they're all on that.

25

PLAYBOY: "And I Love Her."

LENNON: "And I Love Her" is Paul again. I consider it his first "Yesterday." You know, the big ballad in *Hard Day's Night*. The middle eight, I helped with that.

PLAYBOY: "I'll Be Back."

LENNON: "I'll Be Back" is me completely. My variation of the chords in a Del Shannon song.

PLAYBOY: "World Without Love."

LENNON: McCartney. I think that might have been another one. . . . He had quite a lot of material already . . . he was already more of a songwriter than me when we met. So I think that was also resurrected from the past. I don't know, I think he had the whole song before Beatles and gave it to Peter and Gordon, one of whom is now the famous Peter Asher. I don't know what became of Gordon. Paul never sang it. Not on a record, anyway. That has the line "Please lock me away"—which we always used to crack up at. . . .

PLAYBOY: "One and One Is Two."

LENNON: That's another of Paul's bad attempts at writing a song.

PLAYBOY: "I Feel Fine."

LENNON: That's me completely. Including the electric guitar lick *and* the record with the first feedback anywhere. I defy anybody to find a record—unless it's some old blues record in 1922—that uses feedback that way. I mean, everybody played with feedback on stage, and the Jimi Hendrix stuff was going on long before. In fact, the punk stuff now is only what people were doing in the clubs. So I claim it for the Beatles. Before Hendrix, before The Who, before anybody. The first feedback on any record.

PLAYBOY: "She's a Woman."

LENNON: That's Paul with some contribution from me on lines, probably. We put in the words "turns me on." We were so excited to say "turn me on"—you know, about marijuana and all that, using it as an expression.

PLAYBOY: "No Reply."

LENNON: That's my song. That's the one where Dick James, the publisher, said, "That's the first complete song you've written where it resolves itself." You know, with a complete story. It was sort of my version of "Silhouettes." [*Singing*] "Silhouettes, silhouettes, silhouettes . . ." I had that image of walking down the street and seeing her silhouetted in the window and not answering the phone, although I never called a girl on the phone in my *life*. Because phones weren't part of the English child's life.

PLAYBOY: "I'll Follow the Sun."

LENNON: That's Paul again. Can't you tell? I mean, "Tomorrow may rain so I'll follow the sun." That's another early McCartney. You know, written almost before Beatles, I think. He had a *lot* of stuff. . . .

PLAYBOY: "Eight Days a Week."

LENNON: "Eight Days a Week" was the running title for *Help!* before they came up with "Help!" It was Paul's effort at getting a single for the movie. That luckily turned to "Help!" which I wrote, bam! bam! like that and got the single. "Eight Days a Week" was never a good song. We struggled to record it and struggled to make it into a song. It was his initial effort, but I think we both worked on it. I'm not sure. But it was lousy anyway.

PLAYBOY: Why did they change the movie to *Help!*?

LENNON: Because it was a better title. *Hard Day's Night* was the same. I was going home in the car and Dick Lester suggested the title *Hard Day's Night* from something Ringo'd said. I had used it in *In His Own Write*, but it was an off-the-cuff remark by Ringo. You know, one of those malapropisms. A Ringoism, where he said it not to be funny, just said it. So Dick Lester said we are going to use that title, and the next morning I brought in the song. 'Cause there was a little competition between Paul and I as to who got the "A" side, who got the hit singles.

If you notice, in the early days the majority of singles—in the movies and everything—were mine. And then only when I became self-conscious and inhibited, and maybe the astrology wasn't right, did Paul start dominating the group a little too much for my liking. But in the early period, obviously, I'm dominating the group. I did practically every single with my voice except for "Love Me Do." Either my song, or my voice, or both.

PLAYBOY: Did he—

LENNON: The only reason he sang on "Hard Day's Night" was because I couldn't reach the notes. [*Singing*] "When I'm home, everything seems to be right. When I'm home . . ."—which is what we'd do sometimes. One of us couldn't reach a note but he wanted a different sound, so he'd get the other to do the harmony.

PLAYBOY: Was there resentment from Paul at first?

LENNON: No, it wasn't resentment, but it *was* competitive. But I had "Please Please Me," most of "She

Loves You,'' most of "From Me to You," all my voice. What comes after that? Let me think. . . . Well, whatever. You know, you just listen to early Beatles and you'll hear it. "I Want to Hold Your Hand": Again, I was the lead voice on that. So up to that period it was mainly my domination on the record scene. Although I *never* dominated the fan worship because the kids . . . the girls always went for him. Mine was a male following more than a female following.

PLAYBOY: So after they changed *Eight Days a Week*, the movie, to *Help!* . . .

LENNON: I remember Maureen Cleave, a writer—the one who did the famous "We're-more-popular-than-Jesus" story in the *Evening Standard*—asked me, "Why don't you ever write songs with more than one syllable?" So in "Help!" there are two- or three-syllable words and I very proudly showed them to her and she still didn't like them. I was insecure then, and things like that happened more than once. I never considered it before. So after that I put a few words with three syllables in, but she didn't think much of them when I played it for her, anyway.

PLAYBOY: Was there anything in particular that inspired *Help!*?

LENNON: Well, it was 1965. The movie was out of our control. With *Hard Day's Night*, we pretty much had a lot of input, and it was semirealistic. But with *Help!*, Dick didn't tell us what it was about, though I realize, looking back, how advanced it was. It was a precursor for the "Batman" "Pow! Wow!" on TV—that kind of stuff. But he never explained it to us. Partly, maybe, because we hadn't spent a lot of time together between *Hard Day's Night* and *Help!* And partly because by then we were smoking marijuana for breakfast during that period. Nobody could communicate with us because it was all glazed eyes and giggling all the time. In our own world.

The whole Beatle thing was just beyond comprehension. I was eating and drinking like a pig and I was fat as a pig, dissatisfied with myself, and subconsciously I was crying for help. I think everything comes out in the songs, even Paul's songs now, which are apparently about nothing. The same way as handwriting analysis shows everything about yourself. Or Dylan, trying to hide in the subterfuge of clever hippie words, but it was always apparent—if you looked below the surface—what was being said. Resentfulness, or love, or hate—it's apparent in all work. It's just harder to see when it's written in gobbledy-gook.

When *Help!* came out, I was actually crying out for help. Most people think it's just a fast rock 'n' roll song. I didn't realize it at the time; I just wrote the song because I was commissioned to write it for the movie. But later, I knew I really was crying out for help. So it was my fat Elvis period. You see the movie: He—I—is very fat, very insecure, and he's completely lost himself. And I am singing about when I was so much younger and all the rest, looking back at how easy it was. Now I may be very positive—yes, yes—but I also go through deep depressions where I would like to jump out the window, you know. It becomes easier to deal with as I get older; I don't know whether you learn control or, when you grow up, you calm down a little. Anyway, I was fat and depressed and I *was* crying out for help.

PLAYBOY: Moving on: "It's Only Love."

LENNON: "It's Only Love" is mine. I always thought it was a lousy song. The lyrics were abysmal. I always hated that song.

PLAYBOY: "Yesterday."

LENNON: "Yesterday" . . . Well, we know all about "Yesterday." I have had *so* much accolade for "Yesterday." That's Paul's song and Paul's baby. Well done. Beautiful—and I never wished I'd written it.

PLAYBOY: "Day Tripper."

LENNON: That's mine. Including the lick, the guitar break and the whole bit. It's just a rock 'n' roll song. Day trippers are people who go on a day trip, right?

Usually on a ferryboat or something. But it was kind of—you know, you're just a weekend hippie. Get it?

PLAYBOY: "We Can Work It Out."

LENNON: In "We Can Work It Out," Paul did the first half, I did the middle eight. But you've got Paul writing, "We can work it out/We can work it out"—real optimistic, y'know, and me, impatient: "Life is very short and there's no time/For fussing and fighting, my friend. . . ."

PLAYBOY: Paul tells the story and John philosophizes.

LENNON: Sure. Well, I was always like that, you know. I was like that before the Beatles and after the Beatles. I always asked why people did things and why society was like what it was. I didn't just accept it for what it was *apparently* doing. I always looked below the surface.

PLAYBOY: "Norwegian Wood."

LENNON: "Norwegian Wood" is my song completely. It was about an affair I was having. I was very careful and paranoid because I didn't want my wife, Cyn, to know that there really was something going on outside of the household. I'd always had *some* kind of affairs going, so I was trying to be sophisticated in writing about an affair. But in such a smoke-screen way that you couldn't tell. But I can't remember any specific woman it had to do with.

PLAYBOY: What about the title itself?

LENNON: I don't know *how* the hell I got to "Norwegian Wood."

PLAYBOY: "What Goes On."

LENNON: That was an early Lennon written before Beatles when we were the Quarrymen, or something like that. And resurrected with a middle eight thrown in, probably with Paul's help, to give Ringo a song and also to use the bits, because I never liked to waste anything.

PLAYBOY: Let's see . . . "In My Life" we talked about—

LENNON: For "In My Life," I had a complete set of

lyrics after struggling with a journalistic version of a trip from home to downtown on a bus naming every sight. It became "In My Life," which is a remembrance of friends and lovers of the past. Paul helped with the middle eight musically. But all lyrics written, signed, sealed, and delivered. And it was, I think, my first real major piece of work. Up till then it had all been sort of glib and throwaway. And that was the first time I consciously put my literary part of myself into the lyric. Inspired by Kenneth Alsopf, the British journalist, and Bob Dylan.

PLAYBOY: "Run for Your Life."

LENNON: "Run for Your Life." Just a sort of throwaway song of mine that I never thought much of, but it was always a favorite of George's.

PLAYBOY: Doesn't that have a line you actually took from another rock 'n' roll song?

LENNON: Yeah, it has a line from an old Presley song: "I'd rather see you dead, little girl, than to be with another man" is a line from an old blues song that Presley did once.

PLAYBOY: "Paperback Writer."

LENNON: "Paperback Writer" is son of "Day Tripper," but it is Paul's song.

PLAYBOY: Son of "Day Tripper" meaning . . .

LENNON: Meaning a rock 'n' roll song with a guitar lick on a fuzzy, loud guitar.

PLAYBOY: "Eleanor Rigby." We talked about that.

LENNON: Well, we covered that, right? Paul's baby, and I helped with the education of the child.

PLAYBOY: "Here, There and Everywhere."

LENNON: Paul's song completely, I believe. And one of my favorite songs of the Beatles.

PLAYBOY: "Yellow Submarine."

LENNON: "Yellow Submarine" is Paul's baby. Donovan helped with the lyrics. I helped with the lyrics, too. We virtually made the track come alive in the studio, but based on Paul's inspiration. Paul's idea, Paul's title. So I count it as a "Paul" song.

PLAYBOY: And Ringo sang it, right?

LENNON: Yeah. Written for Ringo.

PLAYBOY: "She Said, She Said."

LENNON: That's mine. It's a—an interesting track. The guitars are great on it. That was written after an acid trip in L.A. during a break in the Beatles' tour where we were having fun with the Byrds and lots of girls. Some from PLAYBOY, I believe. Peter Fonda came in when we were on acid and he kept coming up to me and sitting next to me and whispering, "I know what it's like to be dead."

He was describing an acid trip he'd been on. We didn't *want* to hear about that! We were on an acid trip and the sun was shining and the girls were dancing and the whole thing was beautiful and Sixties, and this guy—who I really didn't know; he hadn't made *Easy Rider* or anything—kept coming over, wearing shades, saying, "I know what it's like to be dead," and we kept leaving him because he was so boring! And I used it for the song, but I changed it to "she" instead of "he." It was scary. You know, a guy . . . when you're flying high and [*whispers*] "I know what it's like to be dead, man." I remembered the incident. Don't tell me about it! I don't want to know what it's like to be dead!

PLAYBOY: "Good Day Sunshine."

LENNON: "Good Day Sunshine" is Paul's. Maybe I threw a line in or something. I don't know.

PLAYBOY: "For No One."

LENNON: Paul's. One of my favorites of his. A nice piece of work.

PLAYBOY: "And Your Bird Can Sing."

LENNON: Another of my throwaways.

PLAYBOY: "Doctor Robert."

LENNON: Another of mine. Mainly about drugs and pills. It was about myself. I was the one that carried all the pills on tour and always . . .

PLAYBOY: Dispensed them?

LENNON: Yeah. Well, in the early days. Later on,

the roadies did it. We just kept them in our pockets loose. In case of trouble.

PLAYBOY: "Got to Get You into My Life."

LENNON: Paul's again. I think that was one of his best songs, too, because the lyrics are good and I didn't write them. You see? When I saw that he could write lyrics if he took the effort, here's an example. It actually describes his experience taking acid. I think that's what he's talking about. I couldn't swear to it, but I think it was a result of that.

PLAYBOY: "Tomorrow Never Knows."

LENNON: That's me in my *Tibetan Book of the Dead* period. I took one of Ringo's malapropisms as the title, to sort of take the edge off the heavy philosophical lyrics.

PLAYBOY: "With a Little Help from My Friends."

LENNON: That's Paul with a little help from me. "What do you see when you turn out the light/I can't tell you but I know it's mine" is mine.

PLAYBOY: "Lucy in the Sky with Diamonds."

LENNON: My son Julian came in one day with a picture he painted about a school friend of his named Lucy. He had sketched in some stars in the sky and called it "Lucy in the Sky with Diamonds." Simple.

PLAYBOY: The other images in the song weren't drug-inspired?

LENNON: The images were from *Alice in Wonderland*. It was Alice in the boat. She is buying an egg and it turns into Humpty-Dumpty. The woman serving in the shop turns into a sheep and the next minute they are rowing in a rowing boat somewhere and I was visualizing that. There was also the image of the female who would someday come save me—a "girl with kaleidoscope eyes" who would come out of the sky. It turned out to be Yoko, though I hadn't met Yoko yet. So maybe it should be "Yoko in the Sky with Diamonds."

It was purely unconscious that it came out to be LSD. Until somebody pointed it out, I never even thought of it. I mean, who would ever bother to look at initials of a title? It's *not* an acid song. The imagery was Alice in the boat. And also the image of this female who would come and save me—this secret love that was going to come one day. So it turned out to be Yoko, though, and I hadn't met Yoko then. But she was my imaginary girl that we all have.

PLAYBOY: "Getting Better."

LENNON: It is a diary form of writing. All that "I used to be cruel to my woman, I beat her and kept her apart from the things that she loved" was me. I used to be cruel to my woman, and physically—any woman. I was a hitter. I couldn't express myself and I hit. I fought men and I hit women. That is why I am always on about peace, you see. It is the most violent people who go for love and peace. Everything's the opposite. But I sincerely believe in love and peace. I am a violent man who has learned not to be violent and regrets his violence. I will have to be a lot older before I can face in public how I treated women as a youngster.

26

The bathroom session ended as John grew tired, suggesting that we leave the work and take a walk. We left the Dakota through the basement and walked down Seventy-second to Columbus and around the block. It was dark and cool, refreshing after the day's intensive interviewing. John rolled his sleeves up high and puffed a cigarette as we strolled and talked. We headed back up Sixty-ninth toward Central Park West, laughing and joking.

John seemed peacefully at ease in the park; the darkness allowed total anonymity. An hour or so later, John guessed Yoko would be finished working for the day. I walked him back to the Dakota.

The next day I met him at the Hit Factory. There, he sang the vocals on "Woman" and background vocals to "Every Man Has a Woman." He sang with his eyes closed to the world's distractions. He swayed and flowed with the music, patiently singing and resinging his parts. When he finished, I joined him in Yoko's room to continue his reflections on the songs.

PLAYBOY: "Being for the Benefit of Mr. Kite"?

LENNON: The whole song is from a Victorian poster, which I bought in a junk shop. It is so cosmically beautiful. It's a poster for a fair that must have happened in the 1800s. Everything in the song is from that poster, except the horse wasn't called Henry. Now, there were all kinds of stories about Henry the Horse being heroin. I had never seen heroin in that period. No, it's all just from that poster. The song is pure, like a painting, a pure watercolor.

PLAYBOY: "When I'm Sixty-Four"?

LENNON: Paul's, completely. I would never even *dream* of writing a song like that. There's some things I never think about, and that's one of them.

PLAYBOY: "Good Morning, Good Morning"?

LENNON: "Good Morning" is mine. It's a throwaway, a piece of garbage, I always thought. The "Good morning, good morning" was from a Kellogg's cereal commercial. I always had the TV on very low in the background when I was writing and it came over and then I wrote the song.

PLAYBOY: You've told the story of this one before, but what about "A Day in the Life"?

LENNON: Just as it sounds: I was reading the paper one day and noticed two stories. One was about the Guinness heir who killed himself in a car. That was the main headline story. He died in London in a car crash. On the next page was a story about four thousand potholes in the streets of Blackburn, Lancashire, that needed to be filled. Paul's contribution was the beautiful little lick in the song, "I'd love to turn you on," that he'd had floating around in his head and couldn't use. I thought it was a damn good piece of work.

PLAYBOY: "Baby You're a Rich Man"?

LENNON: That's a combination of two separate pieces, Paul's and mine, put together and forced into one song. One-half was all mine. [*Sings*] "How does it feel to be one of the beautiful people, now that you know who you are, da da da da." Then Paul comes in with [*sings*] "Baby, you're a rich man," which was a lick he had around.

PLAYBOY: We've mentioned "I Am the Walrus"—

LENNON: Right. The first line was written on one acid trip one weekend, the second line on another acid trip the next weekend, and it was filled in after I met Yoko.

PLAYBOY: Aren't there some lyrics putting down Hare Krishna?

LENNON: I'd seen Allen Ginsberg and some other people who liked Dylan and Jesus going on about Hare Krishna. It was Ginsberg, in particular, I was referring to. The words "Element'ry penguin" meant that it's naïve to just go around chanting Hare Krishna or putting all your faith in one idol.

In those days I was writing obscurely, a la Dylan, never saying what you mean, but giving the *impression* of something. Where more *or* less can be read into it. It's a good game. I thought, *They* get away with this artsy-fartsy crap; there has been more said about Dylan's wonderful lyrics than was ever in the lyrics at all. Mine, too. But it was the intellectuals who read all this into Dylan or the Beatles. Dylan got away with murder. I thought, well, I can write this crap, too.

You know, you just stick a few images together, thread them together, and you call it poetry. Well, maybe it *is* poetry. But I was just using the mind that wrote *In His Own Write* to write that song. There was even some live BBC radio on one track, y'know. They were reciting Shakespeare or something and I just fed whatever lines were on the radio right into the song.

PLAYBOY: What about the walrus itself?

LENNON: It's from "The Walrus and the Carpenter." *Alice in Wonderland*. To me, it was a beautiful poem. It never dawned on me that Lewis Carroll was commenting on the capitalist system. I never went into that bit about what he really meant, like people are doing with the Beatles' work. Later, I went back and looked at it and realized that the walrus was the bad guy in the story and the carpenter was the good guy. I thought, Oh, shit, I picked the wrong guy. I should have said, "I am the carpenter." But that wouldn't have been the same, would it? [*Sings, laughing*] "I am the carpenter . . ."

PLAYBOY: "Magical Mystery Tour"?

LENNON: Paul's song. Maybe I did part of it, but it was his concept.

PLAYBOY: Was the entire album of that name his concept, too?

LENNON: Yeah . . . and there was a problem with that period, which is why I got a little resentful later on about the album. I was living a more suburban life at the time, with a wife and a kid, while he was still tripping around town, hanging out and being a bachelor. He'd work something out for a song or an album and then suddenly call me and say, "It's time to go into the studio. Write some songs." He'd have all *his* prepared, ready with ideas and arrangements, while I would be starting from scratch.

On *Sgt. Pepper*, which was his idea, too, I managed to come up with "Lucy in the Sky" and "Day in the Life" under the pressure of only ten days. Even so, I was in more at the start. But later on, I had sort of succumbed to marriage and eating. On the *Mystery Tour* album I only had two songs as well—"I Am the Walrus" and "Strawberry Fields." I didn't have time to write anything else. He'd already written *twenty* songs, or whatever the hell there is on that album. George just barely managed to get on. Luckily "Walrus" and "Strawberry Fields" were so fantastic everybody remembers that—and "Fool on the Hill," which was Paul's major. Now that's Paul. Another good lyric. Shows he's capable of writing complete songs.

PLAYBOY: Back to *Sgt. Pepper:* How about George's "Within You, Without You"?

LENNON: One of George's best songs. One of my favorites of his, too. He's clear on that song. His mind and his music are clear. There is his innate talent; he brought that sound together.

PLAYBOY: "Hey Jude."

LENNON: "Hey Jude" is Paul's. It's one of his masterpieces.

PLAYBOY: You had nothing to do with it?

LENNON: I don't think I had anything to do with it. He said it was written about Julian, my child. He knew I was splitting with Cyn and leaving Julian. He was driving over to say hi to Julian. He'd been like an uncle to him. You know, Paul was always good with kids. And so he came up with "Hey Jude."

But I always heard it as a song to me. If you think about it : . . Yoko's just come into the picture. He's saying, "Hey, Jude—hey, John." I know I'm sounding like one of those fans who reads things into it, but you *can* hear it as a song to me. The words "go out and get her"—subconsciously he was saying, Go ahead, leave me. On a conscious level, he didn't want me to go ahead. The angel in him was saying, "Bless you." The devil in him didn't like it at all, because he didn't want to lose his partner.

PLAYBOY: "Revolution."

LENNON: Completely me. We recorded the song twice. The Beatles were getting real tense with each other. I did the slow version and I wanted it out as a single: as a statement of the Beatles' position on Vietnam and the Beatles' position on revolution. For years, on the Beatles' tours, Brian Epstein had stopped us from saying anything about Vietnam or the war. And he wouldn't allow questions about it. But on one of the last tours, I said, "I am going to answer about the war. We can't ignore it.'' I *absolutely* wanted the Beatles to say something about the war.

The first take of "Revolution"—well, George and Paul were resentful and said it wasn't fast enough. Now, if you go into the details of what a hit record is and isn't, maybe. But the Beatles could have afforded to put out the slow, understandable version of "Revolution" as a single, whether it was a gold record or a wooden record. But because they were so upset over the Yoko thing and the fact that I was again becoming as creative and dominating as I had been in the early days, after lying fallow for a couple of years, it upset the applecart. I was awake again and they weren't used to it.

PLAYBOY: Was it Yoko's inspiration?

LENNON: She inspired *all* this creation in me. It wasn't that she inspired the songs; she inspired *me*. The statement in "Revolution" was mine. The lyrics stand today. They're still my feeling about politics: I want to see the *plan*. That is what I used to say to Jerry Rubin and Abbie Hoffman. Count me out if it's for violence. Don't expect me on the barricades unless it is with flowers. As far as overthrowing something in the name of Marxism or Christianity, I want to know what you're going to do *after* you've knocked it all down. I mean, can't we use *some* of it? What's the point of bombing Wall Street? If you want to change the system, change the system. It's no good shooting people.

27

PLAYBOY: What do you remember about "Revolution 9"?

LENNON: Well, the slow version of "Revolution" on the album went on and on and on and I took the fade-out part, which is what they sometimes do with disco records now, and just layered all this stuff over it. It has the basic rhythm of the original "Revolution" going on with some twenty loops we put on, things from the archives of EMI. We were cutting up classical music and making different-size loops, and then I got an engineer tape on which some test engineer was saying, "Number nine, number nine, number nine." All those different bits of sound and noises are all compiled. There were about ten machines with people holding pencils on the loops—some only inches long and some a yard long. I fed them all in and mixed them live. I did a few mixes until I got one I liked. Yoko was there for the whole thing and she made decisions about which loops to use. It was somewhat under her influence, I suppose. Once I heard her stuff—not just the screeching and the howling but her sort of word pieces and talking and breathing and all this strange stuff, I thought, My God, I got intrigued, so I wanted to do one. I spent more time on "Revolution 9" than I did on half the other songs I ever wrote. It was a montage.

PLAYBOY: "Back in the USSR."

LENNON: Paul completely. I play the six-string bass on that. [*Sings as he pretends to play bass guitar*] "Da da da da da . . ." Try writing *that* on your typewriter.

PLAYBOY [*laughing*]: Thanks. "Happiness Is a Warm Gun"?

LENNON: Me completely.

PLAYBOY: And it's not about drugs?

LENNON: No. A gun magazine was sitting around and the cover was the picture of a smoking gun. The title of the article, which I never read, was "Happiness Is a Warm Gun." I took it as the idea of happiness after having shot somebody. Or some animal.

PLAYBOY: It wasn't a sexual thing? "When I hold you in my arms/And I feel my hand on your trigger"?

LENNON: Oh, well, by then I'm into double meanings. The initial inspiration was from the magazine cover. But that was the beginning of my relationship with Yoko and I was very sexually oriented then. When we weren't in the studio, we were in bed.

PLAYBOY: What about the allusion to "Mother Superior jumps the gun"?

LENNON: I call Yoko Mother or Madam just in an offhand way. The rest doesn't mean anything. It's just images of her.

PLAYBOY: "Rocky Raccoon."

LENNON: Paul. Couldn't you guess? Would I go to all that trouble about Gideon's Bible and all that stuff?

PLAYBOY: "Why Don't We Do It in the Road?"

LENNON: That's Paul. He even recorded it by himself in another room. That's how it was getting in those days. We came in and he'd made the whole record. Him drumming. Him playing the piano. Him singing. But he couldn't—he couldn't—maybe he couldn't make the break from the Beatles. I don't know what it was, you know. I enjoyed the track. Still, I can't speak for George, but I was always hurt when Paul would knock something off without involving us. But that's just the way it was then.

PLAYBOY: You never just knocked off a track by yourself?

LENNON: No.

PLAYBOY: "Julia."

LENNON: That was mine.

PLAYBOY: Who was Julia?

LENNON: Julia was my mother. But it was sort of a combination of Yoko and my mother blended into one. That was written in India. On "the white album" [*The Beatles*]. And all the stuff on "the white album" was written in India while we were supposedly giving money to Maharishi, which we never did. We got our mantra, we sat in the mountains eating lousy vegetarian food and writing all those songs. We wrote *tons* of songs in India.

PLAYBOY: Including "Birthday"?

LENNON: No. "Birthday" was written in the studio. Just made up on the spot. I think Paul wanted to write a song like "Happy Birthday Baby," the old Fifties hit. But it was sort of made up in the studio. It was a piece of garbage.

PLAYBOY: While we're talking about albums, do you have any favorites?

LENNON: No. I like different songs from different albums. I'm not an album person. I really am not. There have only been two great albums that I listened to all the way through when I was about sixteen. One was Carl Perkins's first or second, I can't remember which. And one was Elvis's first. Those are the only ones on which I really enjoyed every track. And I can't . . . as I said, I'm not satisfied with any individual or Beatle album. There's too many fill-ins and paddings. I like the inspired stuff, not the created, clever stuff.

But I do like *Pepper* for what it is. I like "the white album" for what that is, and I like *Revolver* and I like *Rubber Soul*. So there aren't many others, are there? I also like our first album because we made it in twelve hours.

PLAYBOY: All right. What about "Everybody's Got Something to Hide Except"—

LENNON: "Me and My Monkey." That was just a sort of a nice line that I made into a song. It was about me and Yoko. Everybody seemed to be paranoid except for us two, who were in the glow of love. Everything is clear and open when you're in love. Everybody was sort of tense around us: You know, "What is *she* doing here at the session? Why is she with him?" All this sort of madness is going on around us because we just happened to want to be together all the time.

PLAYBOY: "Sexy Sadie."

LENNON: That was inspired by Maharishi. I wrote it when we had our bags packed and we were leaving. It was the last piece I wrote before I left India. I just called him "Sexy Sadie." Instead of [*singing*] "Maharishi, what have you done, you made a fool of . . ." I was just using the situation to write a song, rather calculatingly but also to express what I felt. I was leaving Maharishi with a bad taste. You know, it seems that my partings are always not as nice as I'd like them to be.

PLAYBOY: "Because."

LENNON: Yoko was playing "Moonlight Sonata" on the piano. She was classically trained. I said, "Can you play those chords backwards?" and wrote "Because" around them. The lyrics speak for themselves; they're clear. No bullshit. No imagery, no obscure references.

PLAYBOY: "Across the Universe"?

LENNON: I was a bit more artsy-fartsy there. I was lying next to me first wife in bed, you know, and I was irritated. She must have been going on and on about something and she'd gone to sleep and I'd kept hearing these words over and over, flowing like an endless stream. I went downstairs and it turned into sort of a cosmic song rather than an irritated song; rather than a "Why are you always mouthing off at me?" or whatever, right? But the Beatles didn't make a good record of it. I think subconsciously sometimes we—I say "we," though I think Paul did it more than the rest of us; Paul would . . . sort of subconsciously try and destroy a great song.

PLAYBOY: [*Whistle of surprise.*]

LENNON: Okay?

PLAYBOY: Yes.

LENNON: He subconsciously tried to destroy songs,

meaning that we'd play experimental games with my great pieces, like "Strawberry Fields"—which I always felt was badly recorded. That song got away with it and it worked. But usually we'd spend hours doing little detailed cleaning-ups of Paul's songs; when it came to mine, especially if it was a great song like "Strawberry Fields" or "Across the Universe," somehow this atmosphere of looseness and casualness and experimentation would creep in. Subconscious sabotage. *He'll* deny it 'cause he's got a bland face and he'll say the sabotage doesn't exist. But this is the kind of thing I'm talking about, where I was always *seeing* what was going on. . . . I begin to think, well maybe I'm paranoid. But it's *not* paranoid; it's *absolute* truth.

The same thing happened to "Across the Universe." It was a *lousy* track of a great song and I was so disappointed by it. It never went out as the Beatles; I gave it to the Wildlife Fund of Great Britain, and then when Phil Spector was brought in to produce *Let It Be*, he dug it out of the Beatles files and overdubbed it. The guitars are out of tune and I'm singing out of tune 'cause I'm psychologically destroyed and nobody's supporting me or helping me with it and the song was never done properly.

PLAYBOY: Whew! OK.

LENNON: But the words stand, luckily, by themselves. They were purely inspirational and were given to me as *boom!* I don't own it, you know; it came through like that. I don't know where it came from, what meter it's in, and I've sat down and looked at it and said, "Can I write another one with this meter?" It's so interesting: "Words are flying out like [*sings*] endless rain into a paper cup, they slither while they pass, they slip across the universe." Such an extraordinary meter and I can never repeat it! It's not a matter of craftsmanship; it wrote itself. It *drove* me out of bed. I didn't want to write it, I was just slightly irritable and I went downstairs and I couldn't get to sleep until I put it on paper, and then I went to sleep.

PLAYBOY: Was it like a catharsis?

LENNON: It's like being *possessed;* like a *psychic* or a *medium*. The thing *has* to go down. It won't let you sleep, so you *have* to get up, *make* it into something, and then you're allowed to sleep. That's always in the middle of the bloody night, when you're half awake or tired and your critical facilities are switched off.

"Nowhere Man" was the same thing. I'd spent *five* hours that morning trying to write a song that was meaningful and good and I finally gave up and lay down. Then "Nowhere Man" came, words and music, the *whole* damn thing, as I lay down. The same with "In My Life"! I'd struggled for days and hours trying to write clever lyrics. Then I *gave* up and "In My Life" came to me. So letting it *go* is what the whole game is. You put your finger on it, it slips away, right? You know, you turn the lights on and the cockroaches run away; you can never grasp them.

PLAYBOY: Back to some earlier songs. "There's a Place"?

LENNON: "There's a Place" was my attempt at a sort of Motown, black thing. It says the usual Lennon things: "In my mind there's no sorrow . . ." It's all in your mind.

PLAYBOY: "This Boy"?

LENNON: Just my attempt at writing one of those three-part-harmony Smokey Robinson songs. Nothing in the lyrics; just a sound and harmony.

PLAYBOY: "All I've Got to Do"?

LENNON: That's me trying to do Smokey Robinson again.

PLAYBOY: "Not a Second Time"?

LENNON: That's me trying to do something. I don't remember. [*Laughs*]

PLAYBOY: "I Saw Her Standing There."

LENNON: That's Paul doing his usual good job of producing what George Martin used to call a "potboiler." I helped with a couple of the lyrics.

PLAYBOY: "Tip of My Tongue"?

LENNON: That's another piece of Paul's garbage, not my garbage.

PLAYBOY: "I'll Keep You Satisfied"?

LENNON: Paul.

PLAYBOY: "Nobody I Know"?

LENNON: Paul again. That was his Jane Asher period, I believe.

PLAYBOY: "Things We Said Today"?

LENNON: Paul's. Good song.

PLAYBOY: "You Can't Do That"?

LENNON: That's me doing Wilson Pickett. You know, a cowbell going four in the bar, and the chord going *chatoong!*

PLAYBOY: "Don't Want to See You Again"?

LENNON: That's Paul.

PLAYBOY: "I'm Down"?

LENNON: That's Paul, with a little help from me, I think.

PLAYBOY: "The Night Before"?

LENNON: That's Paul again. I'll just say it's Paul, meaning I don't remember anything about it except it was in the movie *Help!*

PLAYBOY: "I Should Have Known Better"?

LENNON: That's me. Just a song; it doesn't mean a damn thing.

PLAYBOY: "If I Fell"?

LENNON: That's my first attempt at a ballad proper. That was the precursor to "In My Life." It has the same chord sequences as "In My Life": D and B minor and E minor, those kind of things. And it's semiautobiographical, but not consciously. It shows that I wrote sentimental love ballads, silly love songs, way back when.

PLAYBOY: "I'm Happy Just to Dance with You"?

LENNON: That was written for George. I couldn't a sung it.

PLAYBOY: "Tell Me Why"?

LENNON: "Tell Me Why" . . . They needed another

upbeat song and I just knocked it off. It was like a black-New York-girl group song.

PLAYBOY: "Any Time at All"?

LENNON: An effort at writing "It Won't Be Long." Same ilk: C to A minor, C to A minor—with me shouting.

PLAYBOY: "I'll Cry Instead"?

LENNON: I wrote that for *Hard Day's Night*, but Dick Lester didn't even want it. He resurrected "Can't Buy Me Love" for that sequence instead. I like the middle eight to that song, though—that's about all I can say about it.

PLAYBOY: "When I Get Home"?

LENNON: That's me again, another Wilson Pickett, Motown sound, a four-in-the-bar cowbell song.

PLAYBOY: "I'm a Loser"?

LENNON: That's me in my Dylan period.

PLAYBOY: Was that a personal statement?

LENNON: Part of me suspects I'm a loser and part of me thinks I'm God almighty. [*Laughs*]

PLAYBOY: "Another Girl"?

LENNON: "Another Girl" is Paul.

PLAYBOY: "Tell Me What You See"?

LENNON: That's Paul.

PLAYBOY: "I've Just Seen a Face"?

LENNON: That's Paul.

PLAYBOY: "That Means a Lot"?

LENNON: That's Paul.

PLAYBOY: "I Don't Want to Spoil the Party"?

LENNON: That's *me!* [*Chuckles loudly*]

PLAYBOY: "Ticket to Ride"?

LENNON: That was one of the earliest heavy-metal records made. Paul's contribution was the way Ringo played the drums.

PLAYBOY: "Yes It Is"?

LENNON: That's me trying a rewrite of "This Boy," but it didn't work.

PLAYBOY: "You Won't See Me"?

LENNON: Paul.

PLAYBOY: ''I'm Looking Through You''?
LENNON: Paul. He must have had an argument with Jane Asher.
PLAYBOY: ''You've Got to Hide Your Love Away''?
LENNON: That's me in my Dylan period again. I am like a chameleon, influenced by whatever is going on. If Elvis can do it, I can do it. If the Everly Brothers can do it, me and Paul can. Same with Dylan.

28

Jack Douglas interrupted us, asking John to listen to a mix of ''Give Me Something.'' Afterward, we continued.

PLAYBOY: ''You're Gonna Lose That Girl''?
LENNON: That's me.
PLAYBOY: ''Fixing a Hole''?
LENNON: That's Paul, *again* writing a good lyric.
PLAYBOY: ''Lovely Rita''?
LENNON: That's Paul writing a pop song.
PLAYBOY: Was there really a Rita, do you know?
LENNON: Nah! He makes 'em up like a novelist. You hear lots of McCartney-influenced songs on the radio now. These stories about boring people doing boring things: being postmen and secretaries and writing home. I'm not interested in writing third-party songs. I like to write about me; 'cause I *know* me.
PLAYBOY: ''Girl''?
LENNON: That's me. Writing about this *dream* girl again—the one that hadn't come yet. It was Yoko.
PLAYBOY: ''Sgt. Pepper''?
LENNON: ''Sgt. Pepper'' is Paul, after a trip to America and the whole West Coast long-named group thing was coming in. You know, when people were no longer

the Beatles or the Crickets—they were suddenly Fred and His Incredible Shrinking Grateful Airplanes, right? So I think he got influenced by that and came up with this idea for the Beatles. As I read the other day, he said in one of his "fanzine" interviews that he was trying to put some distance between the Beatles and the public—and so there was this identity of Sergeant Pepper. Intellectually, that's the same thing he did by writing "He loves you" instead of "I love you." That's just his way of working. *Sgt. Pepper* is called the first concept album, but it doesn't go anywhere. All my contributions to the album have absolutely nothing to do with this idea of Sgt. Pepper and his band; but it works 'cause we *said* it worked, and that's how the album appeared. But it was not as put together as it sounds, except for Sgt. Pepper introducing Billy Shears and the so-called reprise. Every other song could have been on any other album.

PLAYBOY: "Rain"?

LENNON: That's me again—with the first backwards tape on any record anywhere. Before Hendrix, before The Who, before *any* fucker. Maybe there was that record about "They're coming to take me away, ha-ha"; maybe *that* came out before "Rain," but it's not the same thing.

I got home from the studio and I was stoned out of my mind on marijuana and, as I usually do, I listened to what I'd recorded that day. Somehow I got it on backwards and I sat there, transfixed, with the earphones on, with a big hash joint. I ran in the next day and said, "I know what to do with it, I know . . . Listen to this!" So I made them all play it backwards. The fade is me actually singing backwards with the guitars going backwards. [*Singing backwards*] Sharethsmnowthsmeaness . . . [*Laughter*] That one was the gift of God, of Ja, actually, the god of marijuana, right? So Ja gave me that one.

PLAYBOY: "Hello Goodbye"?

LENNON: That's another McCartney. Smells a mile

away, doesn't it? An attempt to write a single. It wasn't a great piece; the best bit was the end, which we all ad-libbed in the studio, where I played the piano. Like one of my favorite bits on "Ticket to Ride," where we just threw something in at the end.

PLAYBOY: "Your Mother Should Know"?

LENNON: Guess who? Paul.

PLAYBOY: "I'm Only Sleeping"? One of my favorites.

LENNON: It's got backwards guitars, too. That's me—dreaming my life away.

PLAYBOY: "Fool on the Hill"?

LENNON: Paul. Proving he can write lyrics if he's a good boy.

PLAYBOY: "Step Inside Love"?

LENNON: Guess. Paul.

PLAYBOY: "Ob-la-di, Ob-la-da"?

LENNON: I might've given him a couple of lyrics, but it's his song, his lyric.

PLAYBOY: "Dear Prudence"?

LENNON: "Dear Prudence" is me. Written in India. A song about Mia Farrow's sister, who seemed to go slightly balmy, meditating too long, and couldn't come out of the little hut that we were livin' in. They selected me and George to try and bring her out because she would trust us. If she'd been in the West, they would have put her away.

PLAYBOY: Did you have any luck?

LENNON: Well, we got her out of the house. She'd been locked in for three weeks and was trying to reach God quicker than anybody else. That was the competition in Maharishi's camp: who was going to get cosmic first. What I didn't know was I was *already* cosmic. [*Laughs*]

PLAYBOY: "Glass Onion"?

LENNON: *That's* me, just doing a throwaway song, a la "Walrus," a la everything I've ever written. I threw the line in—"The Walrus was Paul"—just to confuse everybody a bit more. And I thought "Walrus" has now become me, meaning "I am the *one*." Only it didn't mean that in this song.

PLAYBOY: Why a walrus?

LENNON: It could've been "The fox terrier is Paul," you know. I mean, it's just a bit of poetry. It was just thrown in like that.

PLAYBOY: "The Continuing Story of Bungalow Bill."

LENNON: Oh, that was written about a guy in Maharishi's meditation camp who took a short break to go shoot a few poor tigers, and then came back to commune with God. There used to be a character called Jungle Jim and I combined him with Buffalo Bill. It's a sort of teen age social-comment song and a bit of a joke. Yoko's on that one, I believe, singing along.

PLAYBOY: "I'm So Tired"?

LENNON: "I'm So Tired" was me, in India again. I couldn't sleep, I'm meditating all day and couldn't sleep at night. The story is that. One of my favorite tracks. I just like the sound of it, and I sing it well.

PLAYBOY: "Yer Blues"?

LENNON: "Yer Blues" was written in India, too. The same thing: up there trying to reach God and feeling suicidal.

PLAYBOY: "Martha My Dear"?

LENNON [*exasperated*]: Enough said.

PLAYBOY: "Blackbird."

LENNON: Enough said. I gave him a line on that one.

PLAYBOY: Do you like the guitar work there?

LENNON: Yeah, he's good at that stuff, you know. So is John Denver.

PLAYBOY: "I Will"?

LENNON: Paul.

PLAYBOY: And "Cry, Baby, Cry"?

LENNON: Not me. A piece of rubbish.

PLAYBOY: "Good Night"?

LENNON: "Good Night" was written for Julian the way "Beautiful Boy" was written for Sean, but given to Ringo and possibly overlush.

PLAYBOY: "Mother Nature's Son"?

LENNON: Paul. That was from a lecture of Maharishi where he was talking about nature, and *I* had a piece called "I'm Just a Child of Nature," which turned into "Jealous Guy" years later. Both inspired from the same lecture of Maharishi.

PLAYBOY: "Helter Skelter"?

LENNON: That's Paul *completely*. All that Manson stuff was built 'round George's song about pigs and this one, Paul's song about an English fairground. It has nothing to do with anything, and least of all to do with *me*. I gave George a couple of lines about forks and knives and eating bacon.

PLAYBOY: For "Little Piggies"?

LENNON: Yeah.

PLAYBOY: "Honey Pie"?

LENNON: [*Laughs*] I don't even want to think about that.

PLAYBOY: OK, now, "Ballad of John and Yoko"?

LENNON: Well, *guess* who wrote that? I wrote that in Paris on our honeymoon. It's a piece of journalism. It's a folk song. That's why I called it "The Ballad of—"

PLAYBOY: "Come Together"?

LENNON: "Come Together" is *me*—writing obscurely around an old Chuck Berry thing. I left the line in "Here comes old flat-top." It is *nothing* like the Chuck Berry song, but they took me to court because I admitted the influence once years ago. I could have changed it to "Here comes old iron face," but the song remains independent of Chuck Berry or anybody else on earth.

The thing was created in the studio. It's gobbledygook; "Come Together" was an expression that Tim Leary had come up with for his attempt at being president or whatever he wanted to be, and he asked me to write a campaign song. I tried and I tried, but I couldn't come up with one. But I came up with *this*, "Come Together," which would've been no good to him—you couldn't have a campaign song like *that*, right?

Leary attacked me years later, saying I ripped him off. I didn't rip him off. It's just that it turned into

"Come Together." What am I going to do, give it to *him?* It was a funky record—it's one of my favorite Beatle tracks, or, one of my favorite Lennon tracks, let's say that. It's funky, it's bluesy, and I'm singing it pretty well. I like the sound of the record. You can dance to it. I'll buy it! [*Laughs*]

PLAYBOY: "Lady Madonna"?

LENNON: Paul. Good piano lick, but the song never really went anywhere. Maybe I helped him on some of the lyrics, but I'm not proud of them either way.

PLAYBOY: "All Together Now"?

LENNON: Paul. I put a few lines in it somewhere, probably

PLAYBOY: "Get Back"?

LENNON: "Get Back" is Paul. That's a better version of "Lady Madonna." You know, a potboiler rewrite.

PLAYBOY: That one is a real story, though, isn't it?

LENNON: No, I think there's some underlying thing about Yoko in there.

PLAYBOY: Really?

LENNON: You know, "Get back to where you once belonged": Every time he sang the line in the studio, he'd look at Yoko.

PLAYBOY: Are you kidding?

LENNON: No. But maybe he'll say I'm paranoid. You know, he can say, "I'm a normal family man, those two are freaks." That'll leave him a chance to say that one.

PLAYBOY: "I Want You."

LENNON: That's me about Yoko.

PLAYBOY: "Let It Be"?

LENNON: That's Paul. What can you say? Nothing to do with the Beatles. It could've been Wings. I don't know what he's thinking when he writes "Let It Be." I think it was inspired by "Bridge Over Troubled Waters." That's my *feeling,* although I have nothing to go on. I know that he wanted to write a "Bridge Over Troubled Waters."

PLAYBOY: "Maxwell's Silver Hammer"?

LENNON [*laughing*]: That's Paul's. I hate it. 'Cuz all I remember is the track—he made us do it a hundred million times. He did *everything* to make it into a single and it never was and it never could've been, but he put guitar licks on it and he had somebody hitting iron pieces and we spent more money on that song than any of them in the whole album, I think.

PLAYBOY: "You Never Give Me Your Money"?

LENNON: That's Paul. Well, that's not a *song,* you know. *Abbey Road* was really unfinished songs all stuck together. Everybody praises the album so much, but none of the songs had anything to do with each other, no thread at all, only the fact that we stuck them together.

PLAYBOY: "Oh! Darling"?

LENNON: "Oh! Darling" was a great one of Paul's that he didn't sing too well. I always thought that I could've done it better—it was more my style than his. He wrote it, so what the hell, he's going to sing it. If he'd had any sense, he should have let me sing it. [*Laughing*]

PLAYBOY: "She Came in Through the Bathroom Window"?

LENNON: That's Paul's song. He wrote that when we were in New York announcing Apple, and we first met Linda. Maybe she's the one that came in the window. I don't know; *somebody* came in the window.

PLAYBOY: "Mean Mr. Mustard"?

LENNON: That's me, writing a piece of garbage. I'd read somewhere in the newspaper about this mean guy who hid five-pound notes, not up his nose but somewhere else. No, it had nothing to do with cocaine.

PLAYBOY: "Polythene Pam"?

LENNON: That was me, remembering a little event with a woman in Jersey, and a man who was England's answer to Allen Ginsberg, who gave us our first exposure—This is so long—you can't deal with all this. You see, *everything* triggers amazing memories. I met him when we were on tour and he took me back to his apartment and I had a girl and he had one he wanted me to meet. He said she dressed up in polythene, which she *did*. She didn't wear jack boots and kilts, I just sort of elaborated. Perverted sex in a polythene bag. Just looking for something to write about.

PLAYBOY: "Golden Slumbers"?

LENNON: That's Paul, apparently from a poem that he found in a book, some eighteenth-century book where he just changed the words here and there.

PLAYBOY: "Carry That Weight"?

LENNON: That's Paul again. I think he was under strain at that period.

PLAYBOY: "The End"?

LENNON: That's Paul again, the unfinished song, right? We're on *Abbey Road*. Just a piece at the end. He had a line in it [*singing*] "And in the end, the love you get is equal to the love you give," which is a very cosmic, philosophical line. Which again proves that if he wants to, he can think.

PLAYBOY: "One After 909"?

LENNON: That was something I wrote when I was about seventeen. I lived at 9 Newcastle Road. I was born on the ninth of October, the ninth month. It's just a number that follows me around, but, numerologically, apparently I'm a number six or a three or something, but it's all part of nine.

PLAYBOY: "Hey Bulldog"?

LENNON: That's me, 'cuz of the *Yellow Submarine* people, who were gross animals apart from the guy who drew the paintings for the movie. They lifted all the ideas for the movie out of our heads and didn't give us any credit. We had nothing to do with that movie, and we sort of resented them. It was the third movie that we owed United Artists. Brian had set it up and we had nothing to do with it. But I liked the movie, the artwork. They wanted another song, so I knocked off "Hey Bulldog." It's a good-sounding record that means nothing.

PLAYBOY: "Don't Let Me Down"?

LENNON: That's me, singing about Yoko.

PLAYBOY: "Two of Us"?

LENNON: Mine. By the way, Rod Stewart turned "Don't Let Me Down" into [*singing*] "Maggie don't go-o-o." That's one that the publishers never noticed. Why didn't he just *sing* "Don't Let Me Down"? The same reason I don't sing other people's stuff, either: because you don't get paid.

PLAYBOY: "You Know My Name (Look Up My Number)"?

LENNON: That was a piece of unfinished music that I turned into a comedy record with Paul. I was waiting for him in his house, and I saw the phone book was on the piano with the words "You know the name, look up the number." That was like a logo, and I just changed it. It was going to be a Four Tops kind of song—the chord changes are like that—but it never developed and we made a joke of it. Brian Jones is playing saxophone on it.

PLAYBOY: "Long and Winding Road"?

LENNON: Paul again. He had a little spurt just before we split. I think the shock of Yoko and what was happening gave him a creative spurt including "Let It Be" and "Long and Winding Road," 'cuz that was the last gasp from him.

PLAYBOY: "Sun King"?

LENNON: That's a piece of garbage I had around.

PLAYBOY: "Dig a Pony"?

LENNON: Another piece of garbage.

PLAYBOY: "I Get You"?

LENNON: That was Paul and me trying to write a song and it didn't work out.

PLAYBOY: "Baby's in Black"?

LENNON: Together, in the same room.

PLAYBOY: "Every Little Thing"?

LENNON: "Every Little Thing" is his song; maybe I threw something in.

PLAYBOY: "What'cha Doing"?

LENNON: His song; I might've done something.

PLAYBOY: "Baby You Can Drive My Car"?

LENNON: His song, with contributions from me.

PLAYBOY: "The Word"?

LENNON: "The Word" was written together, but it's mainly mine. You read the words, it's all about—gettin' smart. It's the marijuana period. It's love, it's the love-and-peace thing. The word is "love," right?

PLAYBOY: "I've Got a Feeling"?

LENNON: Paul.

PLAYBOY: Since it's sitting here and we gave up on order long ago, how about jumping to the *Rock 'n' Roll* album?

LENNON: It was such a mess that I can hardly remember what happened. I was away from Yoko and I wanted to come back. I did, once I got sober; when I was still drunk I would just ramble on or scream abuse at her or beg her to come back, between Dr. Jekyll and Mr. Hyde. I don't know what I was saying or doing half the time.

PLAYBOY: We're back to the separation. Was Yoko right when she said you had to go through what you went through?

LENNON: Of course she was. Unfortunately, she's almost always right, although she doesn't need to remind me of it over and over [*chuckling*]. Jesus, she's a lot smarter than I am—a lot more intelligent. Most women are innately more intelligent than men, I think. And Yoko's specifically bright. I mean, you can see that yourself, and to live with her is to live with a searchlight. It keeps me awake. But sometimes you don't wanna be awake. I mean, it's too much. You wanna be a fool. *I* do.

Well, the record— You see, previous to that album I never let Phil [Spector] take charge of any production. I had always coproduced. But on the *Rock 'n' Roll* album it took me about three weeks to convince him that *I* didn't want to coproduce and I wouldn't be sitting in the driver's seat next to him. I wanted to just be the singer, age fifteen, and sing these old songs I remem-

bered. Then when he finally did take it on, it sort of
. . . well, we both ended up drinking. So I don't
know, it just got into a big madhouse.

Later I was presented with a hundred million hours'
worth of these mad Phil Spector tapes where I'd been
drunk performing, and I salvaged that album, resang a
lot of it, tried to remix down forty guys all playing out
of tune 'cause nobody was in control. And I quickly
knocked off about five or six more tracks with a different group in New York that I'd been working with on
Walls and Bridges. So the last five or six tracks—which
sound completely different if you ever check the album
out—were all done in about four days, you know. Two
a night, like ''Peggy Sue'' and others I really knew
backwards.

It cost a fortune in time and energy and it was the
most expensive album I ever made. And all I thought I
wanted to do was just sing a bit of rock 'n' roll and not
have to produce songs that had something deep to say.
Just to sing ''Be-Bop-a-Lulu,'' you know. It was the
worst time of my life, that record!

PLAYBOY: That's too bad. Doing those old rock songs
could have been fun.

LENNON: Oh, yes, part of me would like to just do
songs that I remember. I remember the old rock songs
better than I remember my *own* songs. If I sat down in a
room and just started playing, if I had a guitar now and
we were just hanging out singing, I would sing all the
early and mid-Fifties stuff—Buddy Holly and all. I
remember those. I don't remember the chords or the
lyrics or *anything* of the Beatles stuff. So my repertoire
is that. I still go back to the stuff the Beatles performed
before they wrote, you see. I would still enjoy doing it.

There is so much of that ''Oh, well, John is supposed
to have things to say.'' I got locked into that business. I
think, because of the way I had been behaving publicly,
people got into the habit of reviewing my life-style and
not my music. So nobody really listened to the album.
It was more, ''That drunken idiot made a record, ha-ha-

ha.'' So I don't think many people really listened to it without seeing a guy with a Tampax on his head. So maybe [*laughs*] in the future . . . If I forget about the way it was made and just hear it, it ain't so bad.

PLAYBOY: What about *Two Virgins*—where you and Yoko are naked on the album cover?

LENNON: Even before we made this record, I envisioned producing an album of hers and I could see this album cover of her being naked because her work was so pure. I couldn't think of any other way of presenting her. It wasn't a sensational idea or anything.

PLAYBOY: What is the story behind the album?

LENNON: Well, after Yoko and I met, I didn't realize I was in love with her. I was still thinking it was an artistic collaboration, as it were producer and artist, right? We'd known each other for a couple years. My ex-wife was away in Italy, and Yoko came to visit me and we took some acid. I was always shy with her, and she was shy, so instead of making love, we went upstairs and made tapes. I had this room full of different tapes where I would write and make strange loops and things like that for the Beatles' stuff. So we made a tape all night. She was doing her funny voices as I was pushing all different buttons on my tape recorder and getting sound effects. And then as the sun rose we made love and that was *Two Virgins*. That was the first time.

PLAYBOY: It caused a bit of a stir.

LENNON: It was *insane!* People got so *upset* by it—the fact that two people were naked.

PLAYBOY: People said you did those things for their shock value.

LENNON: Well, that's ridiculous, you know. Later people started saying, ''They'll do anything for publicity,'' and then when we stopped talking to the press, we became ''recluses,'' but we got more publicity than when we talked to the press. We just stopped talking to the press. The rest of our lives was as busy and full of things happening as it ever was. Our life is quite as interesting without the media as it is with the media.

During that time I was calling myself Greta Hughes or Howard Garbo. The press was more intrigued than when we were talking all the time. "They went here," or "They were sighted there. . . ." It became fun for us to watch because we hadn't gone anywhere or said anything. The press is amazing, really, like the *Plastic Ono* thing.

PLAYBOY: The *Plastic Ono Band* albums by John and Yoko?

LENNON: Right. I'll show you the original picture of the Plastic Ono Band, which is actually four pieces of plastic. The Plastic Ono Band is a conceptual band. There is no Plastic Ono Band. It's just an idea.

The first ad for the Plastic Ono Band consisted of a page out of the English telephone book—it happened to be the Joneses. I said to someone, "Get me a page from the book," and I was handed the Joneses. The ad had the page from the telephone book and said, "You are the Plastic Ono Band." So *we* are the Plastic Ono Band, and the *audience* is the Plastic Ono Band. There is no Plastic Ono Band. People write in and say, "Do you need a guitarist for the Plastic Ono Band?" No, there is no Plastic Ono Band like there is a Beatles or another group. That's why there's never the same musicians twice.

So there was this press opening for the first *Plastic Ono* single, which was "Cold Turkey" or "Give Peace a Chance." There were these tape recorders in these plastic things. We were in a car accident and in the hospital when the press opening of the song was set, so we couldn't be there. Instead, we sent the Plastic Ono Band, which was just these machines that played the records. The press took pictures and they all discussed the Plastic Ono Band. There were the usual questions: "What does it mean?" and especially, "How *dare* they?" But it was in the papers nonetheless. It got across. And that's the Plastic Ono Band. You're in it. Everybody's in it.

PLAYBOY: There were two *Plastic Ono Band* albums—yours and Yoko's.

LENNON: That's right. People don't know about Yoko's because mine got all the attention. The covers are very subtly different. On one, she's leaning back on me; and on the other, I'm leaning on her. We shot the cover ourselves with an Instamatic.

29

PLAYBOY: More songs. "Jealous Guy"?

LENNON: My song, melody written in India. The lyrics explain themselves clearly: I was a very jealous, possessive guy. Toward everything. A very insecure male. A guy who wants to put his woman in a little box, lock her up, and just bring her out when he feels like playing with her. She's not allowed to communicate with the outside world—outside of me—because it makes me feel insecure.

PLAYBOY: You express even your most painful emotions publicly.

LENNON: I made the decision at sixteen or seventeen that what I did, I wanted *everybody* to see. I wasn't going after the aestheticism or the monastery or the lone artist who supposedly doesn't care what people think about his work. I care a *lot* whether people hate it or love it, because it's part of me and it hurts me when they hate it, or hate me, and it's pleasing when they like it. But, as many public figures have said, "The praise is never enough, and the criticism always bites deep." That's just the predicament of being some . . . artist.

PLAYBOY: Have you ever done a piece that was so personal you chose not to release it?

LENNON: Oh, no, no, no. I never keep anything

unless I didn't like the sound of it or it didn't work. But there's nothing in the files . . . I don't have boxes of unreleased stuff at all. Everything I've ever done's out. If I can sing it in the studio, to an engineer, I can sing it to anyone. [*Pause*] I think the really, really delicate, personal stuff—I still don't know how to express it. People think that *Plastic Ono* is very personal, but there are some subtleties of emotion which I cannot seem to express in pop music. Maybe that's why I will search for other ways of expressing myself. I get frustrated about it. Because it is a limiting medium in some ways.

PLAYBOY: Let's go on. What made you write "How Do You Sleep?" which was obviously a bitter song about Paul?

LENNON: Well, it was like Dylan doing "Like a Rolling Stone," one of his nasty songs. It's using somebody as an object to create something. I wasn't really feeling that vicious at the time, but I *was* using my resentment towards Paul to create a song. Let's put it that way.

It was just a mood. Paul took it the way he did because it obviously, pointedly refers to him, and people just hounded him about it, asking, "How do ya feel about it?" But there were a few little digs on *his* albums, which he kept so obscure that other people didn't notice 'em, you know, but *I* heard them. So I just thought, Well, hang up being obscure! I'll just get right down to the nitty-gritty.

PLAYBOY: You wrote, "Those freaks was right when they said you was dead. . . ."

LENNON: Yeah, well, you know, I think he died creatively in a way.

PLAYBOY: "Oh, Yoko." A great song.

LENNON: It's a very popular track, but I was sort of shy and embarrassed and it didn't sort of represent my image of myself as the tough, hard-biting rock 'n' roller with the acid tongue. Everybody wanted it to be a single—I mean, the record company, the public—everybody. But I just stopped it from being a single 'cause of that. Which probably kept it in number two. It never made number one. The *Imagine* album was number one, but the single wasn't. The only number one I've had since I left the Beatles was "Whatever Gets You Through the Night," which was more like a novelty record.

PLAYBOY: "In the middle of the night I call your name. "

LENNON: Yeah, yeah, it's a message to Yoko. Because I couldn't say it in real life. Maybe, I don't know. I mean not real life! Records are real life, but it expresses in song.

PLAYBOY: We talked a lot about the meaning of "Imagine." What inspired the song?

LENNON: Dick Gregory gave Yoko and me a little kind of prayer book. It is in the Christian idiom, but you can apply it anywhere. It is the concept of positive prayer. If you want to get a car, get the car keys. Get it? "Imagine" is saying that. If you can *imagine* a world at peace, with no denominations of religion—not without religion but without this my-God-is-bigger-than-your-God thing—then it can be true. The song was originally inspired by Yoko's book *Grapefruit*. In it are a lot of pieces saying, Imagine this, imagine that. Yoko actually helped a lot with the lyrics, but I wasn't man enough to let her have credit for it. I was still selfish enough and unaware enough to sort of take her contribution without acknowledging it. I was still full of wanting my own space after being in a room with the guys all the time, having to share everything. So when Yoko would even wear the same color as me, I used to get madly upset: We are not the Beatles! We are not fucking Sonny and Cher!

The World Church called me once and asked, "Can we use the lyrics to 'Imagine' and just change it to 'Imagine *one* religion'?" That showed they didn't understand it at all. It would defeat the whole purpose of the song, the whole idea.

The album *Imagine* was after *Plastic Ono*. I call it *Plastic Ono* with chocolate coating.

PLAYBOY: "Mind Games"?

LENNON: It was originally called "Make Love Not War," but that was such a cliché that you couldn't say it anymore, so I wrote it obscurely, but it's all the same story. How many times can you say the same thing over and over? When this came out, in the early Seventies, everybody was starting to say the Sixties was a joke, it didn't mean anything, those love-and-peaceniks were idiots. [*Sarcastically*] "We all have to face the reality of being nasty human beings who are born evil and everything's gonna be lousy and rotten so boo-hoo-hoo. . . ." "We had fun in the Sixties," they said, "but the others took it away from us and spoiled it all for us." And I was trying to say: "No, just keep doin' it."

PLAYBOY: "Tight A$"?

LENNON: Just a throwaway track. I felt like doing that kind of a song. It's a Tex-Mex sound which actually you could play now and it would be *au courant*, but I don't think many people were doing it then.

PLAYBOY: "One Day at a Time"?

LENNON: Well, that's just a concept of life, you know. How to live life. It was Yoko's idea for me to sing it all falsetto.

PLAYBOY: What about "I'm the Greatest"?

LENNON: "I'm the Greatest"? It's the Muhammad Ali line, you know. I couldn't sing it, but it was perfect for Ringo. He could say "I'm the greatest" and people wouldn't get upset. Whereas if I said "I'm the greatest," they'd all take it *so* seriously.

PLAYBOY: That was the song all four Beatles—plus Billy Preston—worked on, though Paul recorded his tracks in London, right? Did you enjoy working with Ringo and George again?

LENNON: Well, yeah, except when George and Billy Preston started saying, "Let's form a group." I was embarrassed when George kept asking me. He was just enjoying the session, and the spirit was very good, but I was with Yoko, you know. We took time out from what we were doing to help out. The very fact that they would imagine I would form a male group without Yoko! It was still in their minds. . . .

PLAYBOY: You did it out of friendship?

LENNON: Yeah! I wouldn't have done it otherwise.

PLAYBOY: Did you ever ask Ringo to play for your albums?

LENNON: Well, he played on *Imagine* and he played on *Plastic Ono Band*.

PLAYBOY: The same reason?

LENNON: Friendship. And I know how he drums! He drums good, so when I want that kinda drumming, he's the one to ask.

PLAYBOY: "Out of the Blue."

LENNON: Well that's just another kinda love song. Nothin' special.

PLAYBOY: "Only People"?

LENNON: That was a failure as a song. It was a good lick, but I couldn't ever get the words to make sense.

PLAYBOY: "I Know, I Know"?

LENNON: Just a piece of nothing.

PLAYBOY: "You Were Here"?

LENNON: I sort of attempted a Latinesque song in a ballad tradition.

PLAYBOY: "Give Peace a Chance"?

LENNON: All we were saying is give peace a chance.

PLAYBOY: Is it a Lennon-McCartney song as it is credited?

LENNON: No, I didn't write it with Paul; but again, out of guilt, we always had that thing that our names would go on songs even if we didn't write them. It was never a legal deal between Paul and me, just an agreement when we were fifteen or sixteen to put both our names on our songs. I'd put his name on "Give Peace a Chance" though he had nothing to do with it. . . . It was a silly thing to do, actually. It should have been Lennon-Ono.

PLAYBOY: Was it written as a song or for the bed-in when you all sang it?

LENNON: Well, after being interviewed for weeks and weeks and weeks, night and day, with Yoko and me talking about peace from our beds, I had those words coming out of my mouth or Yoko's—wherever the hell they came from—and it became a song.

PLAYBOY: "Cold Turkey"?

LENNON: "Cold Turkey" is self-explanatory. It was banned again all over the American radio, so it never got off the ground. They were thinking I was promoting heroin, but instead . . . They're so *stupid* about drugs! They're always arresting smugglers or kids with a few joints in their pocket. They never face the reality. They're not looking at the *cause* of the drug problem. Why is everybody taking drugs? To escape from *what?* Is life so terrible? Do we live in such a terrible situation that we can't do anything about it without reinforcement from alcohol or tobacco or sleeping pills? I'm not preaching about 'em. I'm just saying a drug is a drug, you know. Why we take them is important, not who's selling it to whom on the corner.

PLAYBOY: "Instant Karma"?

LENNON: "Instant Karma": It just came to me. Everybody was going on about karma, especially in the Sixties. But it occurred to me that karma is instant as well as it influences your past life or your future life. There really is a reaction to what you do now. That's what people ought to be concerned about. Also, I'm fascinated by commercials and promotion as an art form. I enjoy them. So the idea of instant karma was like the idea of instant coffee: presenting something in a new form. I just liked it.

PLAYBOY: "Power to the People."

LENNON: Well, that came from a talk with Tariq Ali, who was sort of a "revolutionary" in England and edited a magazine called *Red Mole*. So I felt I ought to write a song about what he was saying. That's why it didn't really come off. I was not thinking clearly about it. It was written in the state of being asleep and wanting to be loved by Tariq Ali and his ilk, you see. I have to admit to that so I won't call it hypocrisy. I couldn't write that today.

PLAYBOY: "Woman Is the Nigger of the World."

LENNON: That's something Yoko said in 1968 in an interview. It was just such a powerful statement, a few years later I turned it into a song. So it's her title and my song. Actually, I think "Woman Is the Nigger of the World" is the first women's liberation song that came out. It was before Helen Reddy's "I Am Woman." I don't know if my lyrics lived up to Yoko's title.

PLAYBOY: "Number Nine."

LENNON: That was a bit of a throwaway. It was based on some dream I had.

PLAYBOY: What about "Happy Xmas"?

LENNON: "Happy Xmas" Yoko and I wrote together. It says, "War is over if you want it." It was still that same message—the idea that we're just as responsible as the man who pushes the button. As long as people imagine that somebody's doing it to them, and that they have no control, then they have no control.

PLAYBOY: "Old Dirt Road"—that was written with Harry Nilsson wasn't it?

LENNON: Yeah. Just to write a song. You know, "Seein' as we're stuck in this bottle of vodka together, we might as well try and do something."

PLAYBOY: "What You Got"?

LENNON: Well, that's talkin' about Yoko. You really don't know what you got till you lose it.

PLAYBOY: "Bless You"?

LENNON: "Bless You" is again about Yoko. I think Mick Jagger took "Bless You" and turned it into "Miss You." [Singing] "Wherever you are, child on a shooting star." The engineer kept wanting me to speed that up—he said, "This is a hit song if you'd just do it fast." He was right. 'Cause as "Miss You" it turned into a hit. I like Mick's record better. I have no ill feelings about it. I think it's a great Stones track, and I really love it. But I do hear that lick in it. Could be subconscious or conscious. It's irrelevant. Music is everybody's possession. It's only publishers who think that people own it.

PLAYBOY: "Surprise, Surprise"?

LENNON: Just a piece of garbage.

PLAYBOY: "Steel and Glass"?

LENNON: I was trying to write something nasty, and I really didn't feel that nasty, but there's some interesting musical stuff on it.

PLAYBOY [*quoting the song*]: "L.A. tan and New York walk"?

LENNON: Yeah, but Allen Klein doesn't *have* an L.A. tan, does he? So it must be sort of a *combination* of resentments. It's about a few people, but it doesn't mean anything.

PLAYBOY: "Nobody Loves You When You're Down and Out"?

LENNON: Well, that says the whole story. I always imagined Sinatra singing that one, I dunno why. He could do a perfect job with it. Ya listenin', Frank? You need a song that isn't a piece of nothing. Here's one for you. The horn arrangement—everything's made for you. But don't ask me to produce it!

PLAYBOY: How about "Ya-Ya"?

LENNON: "Ya-Ya" was a contractual obligation to Morris Levy as a result of the court case.

PLAYBOY: Somebody forced you to write a song?"

LENNON: Um-hmm. It was a humiliation, and I regret havin' to be in that position, but I did it.

PLAYBOY: Wasn't that the one your son Julian played drums on?

LENNON: Yeah.

PLAYBOY: You give Julian due credit—"Starring Julian Lennon."

LENNON: Well, Julian was playing drums, so I just left on the piano and sang "Ya-ya."

PLAYBOY: I was under the impression you still weren't seeing Julian much.

LENNON: Well, no, he's comin' over here shortly now. I see him whenever he gets off school.

PLAYBOY: Has it been hard for him to be John Lennon's kid?

LENNON: Yeah, he has his own . . . Everybody has a cross to bear, and Julian has that cross, and he'll deal with it. He's a clever boy, and as he gets older we can communicate and he'll understand.

PLAYBOY: How about the album *Some Time in New York City*?

LENNON: You see how they banned the picture here. [*He points to a gold seal pasted onto a corner of the album.*] Yoko made this beautiful poster: Chairman Mao and Richard Nixon dancing naked together, you see? And the stupid retailers stuck a gold sticker over it that you can't even steam off. At least you could steam off that Beatles cover. So you see the kind of pressure Yoko and I were getting, not only on a personal level, and the public level, and the court case, and the fucking government, and this, that, and the other, but every time we tried to *express* ourselves, they would ban it, would cover it up, would censor it.

PLAYBOY: Which Beatles album had the steam-off cover?

LENNON: That was a repackage for the Americans called *Yesterday and Today*. The original cover was the Beatles in white coats with figs 'n' dead bits o' meat and dolls cut up. It was inspired by our boredom and resentment at having to do *another* photo session and *another* Beatles thing. We were sick to death of it. Also, the photographer was into Dali and making surreal pictures. That combination produced that cover.

PLAYBOY: Back to the *New York City* LP. These are mostly collaborations with Yoko, aren't they?

LENNON: Right. Let's go over those with Yoko.

PLAYBOY: The ones that are credited to you alone include "New York City."

LENNON: Which one was that?

PLAYBOY: "Standing in the corner/Just me and Yoko Ono . . ."

LENNON: Yeah. "We was waiting for Jerry to land./Up came a man with a guitar in his hand. . . ." The Jerry was Jerry Rubin. The bloke with a guitar was David Peel. You see how the album's represented as a newspaper. Well, the song's a bit of journalese, like "Ballad of John and Yoko." It tells the story.

PLAYBOY: It says, "Well, nobody came to bug us, hustle us or shove us/So we decided to make it our home. . . . If the Man wants to shove us out,/We gonna jump and shout,/The Statue of Liberty said, 'Come!' . . ." Is that why you're in New York?

LENNON: Well, in New York you could walk around, whereas I still couldn't walk around in London. [*Gazing at the album jacket*] Man, it's nice to see this! There's the one [*Live Jam* LP] that we did in London in a ballroom—the U.N. concert. It was great. It was one of these that went on. We did "Cold Turkey" and "Don't Worry, Kyoko," and half of the audience just walked out 'cause it got really far out. And the rest were there staying with us.

I wonder if any of the people who were there became any of the Pretenders or any of the other young punk groups that have the early Lennon-Ono influence. Like I said, the B-52s girl must have studied Yoko's work like a thesis. You know, that also encouraged us to come out and do our thing again, because we hear what we did did not go unheard. We had gotten to the point where we thought, Well, nobody's hearing us.

PLAYBOY: "Don't Worry, Kyoko" was Yoko's song to Kyoko?

LENNON: That's her way of trying to communicate with her daughter. We're sad to say she's still not allowed to see us.

PLAYBOY: How about "John Sinclair"?

LENNON: They wanted a song about "John Sinclair." So I wrote it. That's the craftsman part of me. If somebody asks me for something, I can do it. I can write anything musically. You name it. If you want a style and if you want something for Julie Harris or Julie London, I could write it. But I don't enjoy doing that kind of work. I like to do inspirational work. I'd never write a song like that now.

PLAYBOY: How did collaborations with Yoko work?

LENNON: For lyrics, we'd either do them together or separately. A lot of the music was really free-form. I would just sort of follow her on guitar, or set a rhythm and she would say, "I like that. I can do this over that." She would select from my limited playing and decide what she wanted to use, or I'd give her a lick and she'd just howl.

We decided to call it a day. We found Yoko, who had arrived earlier, sitting behind the control panel in the studio, working on the mix of "Hard Times Are Over" with Douglas. They were ready to wrap it up as well. Yoko asked if I wanted to join them for a cup of tea at home.

Over tea and cake, we discussed a variety of subjects until we heard the then-familiar scuffle of a child's feet scrambling down the hall. Until Sean's bedtime, the evening was devoted to games with paper and scissors and tape.

30

On September 28, I met John and Yoko for what proved to be the final interview session. They were waiting for me at the apartment and suggested we head to La Fortuna for breakfast.

The café was crowded. I noticed a photo of John, Yoko, and Sean on the wall amid an array of pictures of the café-owners' family and friends. Before we sat down, Yoko remembered some business she had forgotten. "I'll meet you back here in a minute," she said. John suggested we sit in the café's back patio. On our way out, we ordered cappuccinos. We found a table in the corner and huddled there over our coffees to talk.

PLAYBOY: Have you firmed up the title of the album?

LENNON: The title *seems* to be *Double Fantasy*, of course, but I don't know, you know. I wouldn't swear to it. You better check at the last minute.

PLAYBOY: Let's start with "(Just Like) Starting Over."

LENNON: Appropriate enough. [*Hums the song*] A la Bing Crosby . . . Well, "Starting Over" and "Cleanup Time" were sorta written on the run after I'd finished all the other work of writing the other ones. They just sort of came. They were like the fun after the work is finished. I was still in Bermuda.

PLAYBOY: You were in a sort of Fifties mood?

LENNON: Yeah. I'd done that music and identified with it—that was my period—but I'd never written a song that sounded like that period. So I just thought, Why the hell not? In the Beatles days that would have been taken as a joke. One avoided clichés. 'Course now clichés are not clichés anymore.

PLAYBOY: "Spread your wings and fly. . . ." No pun?

LENNON [*laughing*]: No. But you know I nearly took the word "wings" out because I thought, Oh, God! They'll all be saying, "What's this about Wings?" It has nothin' to do with Wings.

Our secluded section of the patio was no longer secluded and the sun was hidden behind the neighboring building. John suggested we take our second cup of coffee inside. The café owner joked with him as we passed by the pastry-filled counter: "Too much fresh air no good for you, eh?"

PLAYBOY: How about "Cleanup Time"?

LENNON: It's a piano lick with the words added. It's pretty straightforward if you read the lyrics, right?

PLAYBOY: With a little inspired message: "Show those mothers how to do it. . . ."

LENNON: That's not in the lyric. There's always a scat lyric to some songs. The song came from a talk with Jack Douglas on the phone before I'd met him, before the session. I was in Bermuda and we were talking about the Seventies and that. We were talkin' about cleanin' up and gettin' out of drugs and alcohol and those kinds of things—not me personally, but people in general. He said, "Well, it's cleanup time, right?" I said, "It sure is," and that was the end of the conversation. I went straight to the piano and started boogyin', and "Cleanup Time" came out. I just sang "Show those mothers how to do it" on the track you heard, but it doesn't have anything to do with the song. It's like "Starting Over" had a whole different set of lyrics originally.

PLAYBOY: Did you revise the lyrics to make the story work?

LENNON: Well, I only had a title. That was one of the songs that you have musically done before the lyrics. So then I thought, What is this? What is this about?

PLAYBOY: "The queen is in the countinghouse counting out the money, the king is in the kitchen . . ."

LENNON: Yeah, it's sort of a description of John and Yoko and their little palace, the Palace of Versailles—the Dakota.

PLAYBOY: "I'm Losing You" or "(Afraid I'm) Losing You"?

LENNON: It literally started when I tried to call from Bermuda and I couldn't get through. I was mad as hell and feelin' lost in space and it's . . . just as much a description of the separation period in the early Seventies as that occasion when I physically couldn't get through on the phone.

PLAYBOY: "I know I hurt you then, but, hell, that was way back then, do you still have to carry that cross?"

LENNON: Yoko has an incredible memory. You know, wives will bring back past things. . . .

Yoko found us and sat in the chair I pulled up for her. "What's the matter, you didn't want to go out?" she asked.

"It's noisy out there and the sun wasn't shining, so this is the quietest place," John responded.

I explained that we were going over the songs on the new album.

ONO: Okay, go ahead.

LENNON: . . . So carryin' that cross is whenever she'll bring up something that's been and gone.

PLAYBOY: Yoko, how about "Kiss Kiss Kiss"?

ONO: It's like my other song called "Look Over from My Hotel Window (Age 39)." It's a basic woman feeling, but I'm sure men feel that way, too, once in a while—that basic frustration is not being able to really communicate. In our childhood we were more capable of touching and kissing each other more freely, but even in childhood society has these restrictions. And in the age when the communication media is expanding more and more and there's *big* communication, the individual communication is getting more and more difficult. There's an alienation between individuals. I think women feel the frustration more than men—again, it's the woman, or at least the feminine side of men and women, that is ignored by society—the male society. That side of us is suffering. That side of us is reaching out to be touched, wanting to be held, wanting to communicate.

PLAYBOY: "Kiss Kiss Kiss" is asking for that.

ONO: Right. Exactly.

LENNON [*giggling*]: Oh, so *that's* what it means.

PLAYBOY: The feeling is cabaret-ish or Casbah-ish.

ONO: It's a vaudeville type of feeling. Sort of Kurt Weill.

LENNON: Vaudeville punk. [*Laughter*]

PLAYBOY: How about "Give Me Something"?

ONO: It's the kind of song women can feel. Women are like the minority groups who never feel they are getting enough. Women are in that position. I have that feeling, and it's just expressing that.

Maybe kids on the street feel that same kind of desperation. It's there with women. It's there with *people*—people dying to be fulfilled.

PLAYBOY: "I'm Moving On."

ONO: I think "I'm Moving On" is a very strong song. I think in the sense of "Well, I've had enough. I'm moving on." But it's not about any specific incident. It's just the feeling: "I don't want to play games. I like everything straight." That's a feeling I have had. I'm proud of the song.

PLAYBOY: John, "Beautiful Boy"?

LENNON: Well, what can I say? It's about Sean. It's self-explanatory. The music and the lyrics came at the same time.

PLAYBOY: "Watching the Wheels"?

LENNON: Well, it's a kind of—it's a song version of the love letter from John and Yoko. It's an answer to "What have you been doing?" "Well, I've been doing this—watchin' the wheels."

ONO: It's where you're at now.

LENNON: Right. Thank you, mother.

PLAYBOY [*quoting the lyrics*]: "People say I'm lazy, dreamin' my life away. . . ."

LENNON: Yeah, well, they been saying that all my life. You wanna read my report card? I have them all from school. That's more of John's life story than John and Yoko's. It says, "He's lazy, he's lazy," but I was never lazy. How can you think if you're doing something all the time? When you're eating, eat. When you're painting, paint. When you're sitting, sit. There's a time for sitting and a time for running. And just because my life is half lived in public, people comment on it.

I'm not lazy. I've done more in my life than most people would do in ten. Absolutely! If I never did another damn thing! Even if I wasn't just laying on my back or looking after Sean or doing *anything,* I've still done more work than most people do in their lifetime—even in the ten-year Beatle period. Being a public figure, as I've said, is a twenty-four-hour-a-day job. People wake you up in the middle of the night and ask you to save Peru. When I was in the mountains of Japan, some asshole got the number and woke us up in the middle of the night to try to get us to do a UNICEF concert.

But I'm not running for office. I'm not gonna curtail everything I say to fit some image of myself or to fit some fantasy of somebody else's image of me. I'm not running for office! If you can't stand the heat, get out of the pissoir!

PLAYBOY: Yoko commented that some people keep their public mask on all the time.

LENNON: If I've got a mask on, I've got it in bed and in public. I mean, I'm not that enlightened that I don't lose touch, get off center—I'm not continually hip. I lose it and gain it and lose it and gain it and I just have to deal with it like anyone else. But I do it under scrutiny.

PLAYBOY: Yoko, "I'm Your Angel"?

ONO: Oh, it's a big put-on thing. But at the same time, the lyrics are really not a put-on. It's *presented* in a put-on way. One night, John and I went into a restaurant and had a beautiful, beautiful dinner and we wanted to hurry home because Sean might worry. It was a warm night, I felt good about it, we saw horse carriages in the park—and I just got inspired.

PLAYBOY: Was it somebody's birthday?

ONO: It was written for John and it is around John's birthday.

LENNON: John and Sean's birthday *are* the same day.

ONO: Yes, I know. I am aware of that.

LENNON: At least you don't have a secretary to remind you to send your housewife-husband and his child a flower, right? It hasn't gotten *that* bad—yet. [*Laughing*]

Actually, that's back to "Losing You." Part of what's behind the song was my own insecurity—my own fear that she was so involved in this business that we'd become peripheral to her life. It's insane, when you look back at it, but it's something I felt.

PLAYBOY: "Woman"?

LENNON: Well, that's to Yoko and to all women in a way. My history of relationships with women is very poor—very macho, very stupid, but pretty typical of a certain type of man, which I was, I suppose. a very insecure, sensitive person acting out very aggressive and macho. Trying to cover up the feminine side, which I still have a tendency to do, but I'm learning. I'm learning that it's all right to be soft and allow that side of me out. The image I project is the thing that's not real—you know, the tendency to put on my boots, like you first came in wearing your Frye boots. I tend to put my cowboy boots on when I'm insecure. I'm wobbling down with the little Cuban heels; whereas, now, I'm in my sneakers and I'm comfy.

PLAYBOY: You can always kick somebody with your cowboy boots.

LENNON [*laughing*]: Right. It's a weapon!

PLAYBOY: But you can't run as fast.

LENNON: That's true, that's true. It's insane.

PLAYBOY: Now we're up to "Beautiful Boys."

ONO: That speaks for itself, really. It's a message to men. John and Sean inspired me, but the third verse is about all the beautiful boys of the world. That's sort of like the extension of the idea. I had relationships with men, but it was always "You know where the door is." I didn't really trouble to find out what *their* needs were, what *their* pains were. With John, that changed. He found out my pain, and I had to find out his pain.

PLAYBOY [*quoting again from the song*]: "Please

never be afraid to cry. . . . Don't ever be afraid to fly. . . ."

ONO: Right. The world consists of men and women— there is no denying that. It is important men and women recognize each other and work with each other. It's really a message to men—reaching out to men to understand.

PLAYBOY: John, "Dear Yoko"?

LENNON: What can I say?

PLAYBOY: "Even after all these years—"

LENNON: "—I miss you when you're not here." It says it all. It's a nice track and it happens to be about my wife. Instead of "Dear Sandra," which another singer might write about a woman who may or may not exist, this is about my wife.

PLAYBOY: "Every Man Has a Woman Who Loves Him."

ONO: It's about love, I suppose. When we know something intuitively, we have a tendency to want to escape from it or hide from it. We can't really express our emotions straight. John is pretty good about expressing his emotions in his songs—I think of "Dear Yoko," which is a beautiful song and it says everything in sort of naked words. I'm not that way.

PLAYBOY: Is it true? Does every man have a woman who loves him?

LENNON: Yer mother loves ya, doesn't she? [*Laughs*]

ONO: In the whole world there will always be one person. It's a relief to know that, too. We louse up our chances by escaping from it. We just have to face it. Be open to it.

PLAYBOY: And then there is "Hard Times Are Over (for a While)."

ONO: We talked about it. It's a prayer. I wrote the song in a kind of bad situation—not mentally, just in an environment I had difficulty with. I was very alone. Not lonely, but alone. It was like me against the world— that kind of situation. And it was definitely a prayer. What inspired me, though, was remembering when

John and I went cross country from New York to San Francisco in a car and we had to stop for gas or something in a sort of like nowhere city. While our driver was getting gas, John and I were standing on the corner of the street looking at each other. I didn't know the name of the city or anything. It didn't matter where we were when we looked into each other's eyes.

PLAYBOY: So that's *Double Fantasy*.

ONO: Well—

LENNON: I was saying, who knows? That might not be the title, so you better check.

ONO: It will be.

PLAYBOY: It will be? Okay.

LENNON: Yeah. You heard it from above.

ONO: [*Laughs*]

LENNON: I'm only sayin' that 'cause she's liable to change it. Something could change. Like now I'm in the new studio, or now I'm in the middle of the ocean. Who knows what's going to happen?

These were Lennon's last words on the tapes of the Playboy Interview sessions.

Epilogue

I spoke to him once on the telephone after that. I called a number within the Dakota when the main telephones were out. John never answered the telephone, but when I heard a simple whistle on the other end of the line, unmistakably his, I said I knew it was him. "Very clever," he said.

After the usual questions—How's California? How's New York?—John reminded me that we were to get together in December to continue going over the songs we hadn't covered yet. We wished each other well. He said he looked forward to getting together again. I thanked him.

On December 7, Yoko called to say that she was very pleased with the interview, which had hit the stands the previous day. She said John was also pleased and excited.

The next day, December 8, John was gone.